Retford Revisited

by
Angela and Paul Meads

Published by
Bookworm of Retford
Spa Lane, Retford, Nottinghamshire.
DN22 6EA
01777 869224

ISBN 9780955167423

First printed 2007

Printed and bound by
Burgess Photo Print Ltd
Beehive Street, Retford.

Contents

Acknowledgements

The following people have assisted in the writing of this book by providing information in many forms including interviews, photographs and a variety of ephemera and objects from the past. They are thanked for their support and enthusiasm in helping to record events of yesteryear and for their willingness to share their memories with others.

Les Beevers
Eric Brett
Robin Breddy
Gladys Bussingham
Bill Durham
Barry Exton
June Footitt
Kathleen Freeman
Barry Green
Len and Val Hatton

Betty Liversidge
Chris Nangle
Frank Pettinger
Ken Richardson
Nav Sandhu
Victor Shaw
Bill Taylor
Harry Tomkins
Roger Tuby
John Wilkins

We would also like to thank the staff at the National Fairground Archive, Sheffield, the staff at the Denman Library, Retford, The Retford Times, Christina Jones and the members of Retford Boxing Club for their kind assistance.

Angela and Paul Meads

When Retford became a Postal Town

Retford became a Postal Town on 24th November 1683, almost fifty years after Charles I opened up his Royal Mail service to the public and after Oliver Cromwell had established the General Post Office in 1657. At that time there were no post offices and mail was carried by stagecoach, horse and cart, or by rider, to and from designated inns and hostelries which had staging and stabling facilities. The mail was then delivered to the required address by a messenger.

The former Rushey Inn on the Old Great North Road

In the days when the Great North Road bypassed Retford, mail was dropped off at the Rushey Inn, near Babworth, but in 1766 the road was rerouted so that it passed through Retford town centre. For the road to be a safe and reliable route for merchandise and post it had to be kept in good repair, and so tolls were collected from those who used the road. A turnpike stone can still be seen on Rectory Road although any inscription has long since been worn away.

West Retford Turnpike Milestone, nestling in ivy on Rectory Road.

The rerouting of the Great North Road increased the collection and delivery of mail from three times a week to a daily service. Retford's mail travelled on the London to York mail coach and the coach would leave the White Hart Inn for both cities at around midday.

An archway, to accommodate horse-drawn coaches, at the White Hart Inn on Bridgegate

Gradually, other towns were added to the list of destinations and a postal service to Gainsborough was added in 1824. But in the 1840s, horse-drawn mail coaches were replaced with a faster service from steam trains.

Retford's first Post Office was opened in around 1784, in Bridgegate, near to where Swannacks stands today. The Postmaster was William Gilby whose annual income was £16. Over the next fifty years, the Post Office can be traced to having been on Carolgate and Newgate Street (now Grove Street). For much of this period Miss Elizabeth Barker was the Postmistress. According to the local historian of 1828 (Mr J. Piercy), the postmistress worked long hours, opening at 8am, closing for an hour or two at midday but then opening again until 10pm. In 1834 she fell into a dispute with the Town Clerk for moving her Post Office to Carolgate, (presumably the opposite end to the Market Square).

George V pillar box, Ordsall Park Road

The Town Clerk complained that the Post Office was too far away. Miss Barker did not move her Office, but one later opened in the Market Square in 1841, near to the site of the Broadstone public house, where members of Henry Spencer's family held the position of Postmaster.

More than a hundred years ago
16 Bridgegate was the Retford Post Office

The Post Office moved to Cannon Square in 1864 and from 1877 to 1922 it was at 16 Bridgegate, before it moved to the site that will be familiar to many Retfordians, on Exchange Street.

The Postmaster was Mr William Parker and he received an income of £300 per year.

Former Post Office buildings on Exchange Street, with the Majestic Theatre in the background (2007)

Exchange Street, the former site of the Retford Post Office. (D Taylor)

The Post Office stayed on Exchange Street until 1993, when it was moved to the Co-op building on Carolgate (now the Yorkshire Trading Centre shop) and then to Mill's Newsagents on Spa Lane, near the Bus Station, when the Co-op closed.

Early letters show how the stamping and marking system within the postal service has changed over the centuries The letter shown here, from 1794, shows the town's name stamped on the front and a circular mark showing the year, which was stamped on the letter's arrival in London.

A later letter shows that a 'mileage mark' was added under the town's name, indicating the distance from London; in this case it was 141 miles.

These simple postmarks were used until postage stamps were introduced in 1840. The letter below, posted from Retford in 1845, shows a minimal address and would probably have been collected by the recipient from the Brighton Post Office.

It became necessary to prevent people from reusing paper stamps and so 'obliterators' were used. From 1844, there were numbered hand stamps and the letter above shows that Retford was issued number 638. A separate date stamp was also applied which meant that every letter had to be stamped twice, so by combining the two marks (see below) the postal worker could do the job in half the time!

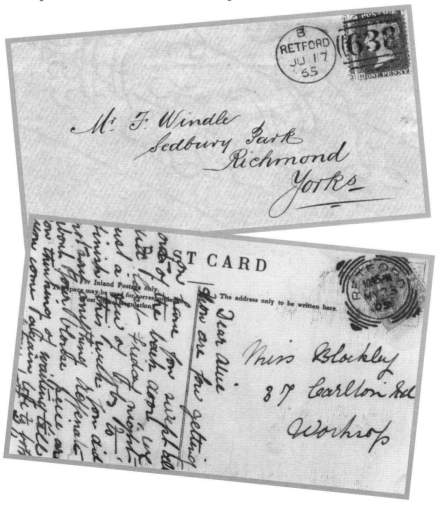

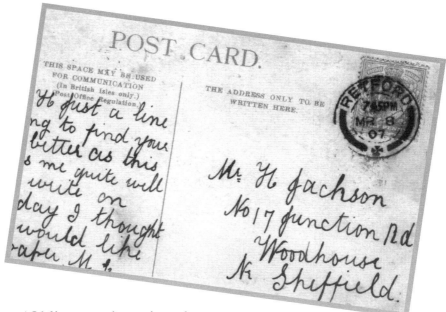

'Obliterators' continued
to evolve in style, as can be seen
by the two postcards shown above. In 1929 all standard
letters posted in Retford had their postage stamps cancelled
by machine.

(All envelopes and postcards curtesy of J.Wilkins).

Retford's Peace Celebrations 1919

The First World War armistice came into effect at 11am on 11 November 1918, the 'eleventh hour of the eleventh day of the eleventh month'.

The Armistice marked the end of fighting on the Western Front, but formal negotiations at the Paris Peace Conference continued into 1919. The Allies' formal peace treaty with Germany, the Treaty of Versailles, was not officially signed until 28 June 1919.

As negotiations continued, the British government planned a public celebration. The Peace Committee was established to decide how Britain would mark the end of the war.
The committee first met in London on 9 May 1919, chaired by the Foreign Secretary, Lord Curzon. Its initial proposal of a four-day August celebration was scaled down and brought forward after the Paris signing. A single day of festivities was planned for 19 July.

The proposal did not receive universal approval. Some felt that the funds would be better spent on support for returning servicemen, many of whom struggled to cope with physical and mental injuries and high unemployment levels.

In Retford, the Saturday market was moved to the preceding Friday and the Mayor made the Peace Proclamation from the Town Hall steps. The town was decorated with flags and bunting, there was a joint street party in East Street (which was on the opposite side of Carolgate across from West

Street and Canal Street (now the site of the West Street car park) and a dance was held on the Cricket Field.

The main celebrations were reserved for 5th August. The Retford, Gainsborough and Worksop Times reported:

RETFORD PEACE CELEBRATIONS
UNITED THANKSGIVING SERVICE
SOLDIERS AND SAILORS ENTERTAINED

The Peace celebrations at Retford passed off in a manner which must be very gratifying to the Mayor and the various committees who, under the able guidance of Mr. John Smith as hon. secretary, worked so hard to make the event one which would live as a red-letter day in the history of the borough. Early on Tuesday morning, when the Mayor and Corporation were assembling in the Council Chamber, there was a steady downpour of rain, and the atmospheric conditions were altogether depressing. But they who profess to be weather-wise predicted that the rain would not last, and for once in a way they were true prophets, for by the time the united service commenced in the Square the rain had ceased. The clouds gradually lifted, and the day turned out to be a perfect one for the sports and gala.

A large crowd assembled in the Market Square for the united religious service which commenced at 11.15. As the discharged and demobilised men assembled in the place allotted to them they were greeted with loud applause. Seats were provided for the disabled men, and one brave hero was wheeled into position in a bath chair. The singing, which was led by the massed choirs from the churches, under the conductorship of Mr. John Smith, was accompanied by the Retford Band.

The assembled were addressed by the Mayor (Sydney Wood), the Lord High Steward of the Borough (Viscount Galway CB ADC), the local Member of Parliament (Sir Ellis Hume-Williams KC), Sir Frederick Milner, Bart. (Bassetlaw M.P. from 1890 to 1906) and Sergeant-Major Johnson (on behalf of the Comrades of the Great War and Federation of Demobilised Soldiers and Sailors).

A souvenir packet of cigarettes presented by the Mayor and Mayoress of Retford (D. Taylor Collection)

It is worth mentioning here that Sir Frederick Milner dedicated himself to improving the lot of disabled war heroes and is remembered as the champion of the ordinary soldier after the First World War. Chiefly through his efforts the administration of pensions was transferred from the commissioners of Chelsea Hospital to a specially created ministry. He also founded the first recuperative hospital for the shell-shocked in Hampstead, London.

> Dinner was then served in the Town Hall, Butter Market and Corn Exchange to the discharged and demobilised men. There were over 1000 present, and it is needless to say that ample justice was done to all the good things provided, and that the men spent a thoroughly enjoyable time.

Fed and watered, everyone moved to the Cricket Field.

> There was a vast crowd on the Cricket Field for the sports and gala. The Retford Band played selections during the afternoon, and an excellent variety entertainment was given by Wil Temple's company of artistes, consisting of conjuring, comedy acrobats and hand balances, juggling, marionettes, comedy sketches, and a Punch and Judy. A capital programme of sports, for which handsome money prizes were offered, had been arranged for the discharged and demobilised soldiers and sailors, and the competition was very keen, the men throwing themselves into the sports in a whole-hearted manner.

To complete the day, in the evening, the band played for dancing in West Retford House grounds, lent for the occasion by Major Milner. But not everyone was grateful.

NO CHILDREN ADMITTED

To the Editor of the "Times"

Sir, - If you can spare me a few lines I should like to air a grievance in connection with the Retford Peace Celebrations. Tuesday's programme informed us, among other items, that dancing would be indulged in, in the evening. Having a desire to witness the terpsichorean display, I with my wife and family made my way to Major Milner's grounds. Imagine my surprise, when I was told by a policeman at the gate that children under 16 years of age would not be admitted. As it was out of the question to leave them outside by themselves, I made my way in alone. Meeting two members of the Town Council, I enquired of them the reason, and was informed that Major Milner did not want children in his grounds because they might damage the garden, etc. If Major Milner did not want children there, why didn't he tell the Peace Committee when he lent them the grounds, in order that they could hold the dancing elsewhere? If Major Milner could have heard a few of the remarks passed by the large crowd of people placed in the same position as myself, perhaps he would have acted differently. It is such small things as these that lead to such rash acts as those which have taken place in other parts of the country - Yours, etc.,

DEMOBBED

The Sherwood Rangers Yeomanry Regiment collect their colours in Retford Market Square 1919 (probably taken by Edgar Welchman)
(D. Taylor collection)

The latter remark relates to events in other towns where the civic authorities failed to respond to the challenges of the post-war period, forgot the sacrifices ordinary servicemen had made, and instead reverted to Victorian values that emphasised civic ritual and deference.

The worst troubles took place in Luton, where the Town Council planned processions with brass bands, floats, entertainment for the children and a fireworks display followed by an evening of official gluttony described as a 'Mayor's banquet'. The cost of the banquet was to be paid from civic funds. Invitations were strictly limited to the Mayor, councillors and close friends - none of whom had served in the armed forces. In fact the officials had not even seen fit to include any ex-servicemen in the preparations, (the Federation wasn't included in Retford's preparations either, until quite late in the day). As a result, the Discharged Soldiers and Sailors' Federation and the Comrades of the Great War Association withdrew from the activities. They had planned alternative celebrations, but the Mayor and his Council refused them the use of a local park.

The three nights of riots that followed the Mayor's reading of the Proclamation of Peace resulted in the burning down of the Town Hall and Luton looking like one of the ravaged cities of World War I. Clearly the returning servicemen felt the country owed them a debt, and who could blame them!

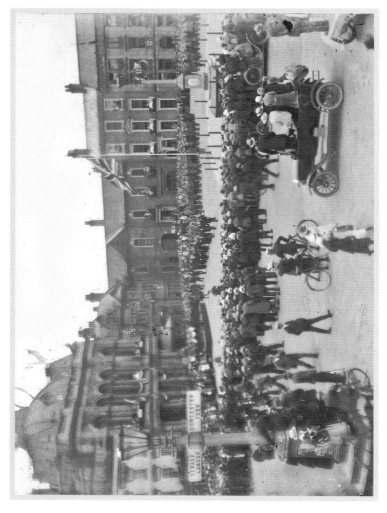

The Sherwood Rangers Yeomanry Regiment collect their colours in Retford Market Square 1919 (probably taken by Edgar Welchman)

(D. Taylor collection)

The final act in the celebrations in Retford took place two days later, on Thursday, 7th August, when the locally raised Sherwood Rangers Yeomanry Regiment collected their Colours, which had been deposited at East Retford Church on 11th August 1914, a week after the declaration of war.

After forming up in the Square, the officers, non-commissioned officers and 600 men who had served with the regiment overseas marched to the Church for a memorial service to remember their fallen comrades.

After reclaiming the Colours, they marched back to the Square, where Viscount Galway, the honorary Colonel of the Regiment, presented Distinguished Conduct Medals to Sergeant Major Tomkins, Sergeant Denman, Corporal Law and Sergeant Bailey, Military Medals to Sergeant Woodcock, Sergeant Walster and Corporal Spring, and the Serbian Cross to Sergeant Woodcock.

The men were then entertained to dinner in the Town Hall and Market Hall, before being dismissed to return to their headquarters in Norfolk.

All The Fun Of The Fair

The modern funfair that visits Retford twice a year, in March and October, marks two significant fair dates that go back hundreds of years. The original fairs would have consisted mainly of the buying and selling of produce such as cheese, hops, fruit, vegetables, sheep and horses. It is not hard to imagine that at these two special times in the year there would also have been street entertainers such as acrobats, jugglers and musicians. Over the years these fairs have evolved and the trading of country produce is no longer a part of them. One of the earliest recorded fairground men who came to Retford was George Thomas Tuby (known as Tom). He arrived in town in 1871 to show his new photographic process.

> The box type camera would be on a tripod, a small container of what had to be a magical liquid to the people of the age, would hang from it. A 'plate' would be taken out of the camera, immersed in the liquid, dried and then fitted to a small mount, before being handed over to a delighted sitter.
>
> *Extract from 'A Showman Supreme'*

Tom introduced other forms of entertainment such as the game of 'Wo Emma' which was named after a popular tune of the day. The 'Emmas' were dolls and by throwing a ball at them, they could be dislodged to win a prize. This was a popular game and soon Tom had £20 to buy his first set of swings and then a coconut shy. By the time he was 30 years old he had his first steam-driven roundabout.

The Market Square, the fairground arrives. Early 1900s

(National Fairground Archive)

One of the most captivating inventions of the 19th century was that of the moving picture and Tom Tuby was quick to respond to this new interest in the days before cinematography.

Tom Tuby decided to bring the cinema to the masses through a bioscope show, as they were called. However, his Coliseum was more than a mere picture show, and this was a good thing. For it is said that these first pictures were so primitive that even the public began to tire of them. But a man like Tom Tuby, a showman supreme, knew that there had to be a total approach to entertainment if he was to succeed against the high competition in the bioscope field.

Extract from 'A Showman Supreme'

A Tuby Family Advertising Rhyme

His gondolas are very fine,
His horses quite a treat.
They're charming to the utmost,
The plant 'tis quite complete.
His Coliseum all should see,
What grandeur meets the eye,
The radiant lights entrancing,
Enthralling to be nigh.
Its exhibition is unique,
'Twill make your grief depart,
'Twill make you really idolize,
And joy to you impart.
Its management if quite superb,
The reins are held by skill,
By Mr. Tuby's clever hand,
Pray come and have your fill.

The Market Square, the fairground arrives. Early 1900s

(National Fairground Archive)

The Coliseum is believed by the family to have been made by Orton and Spooner and the curtain in front of the screen and stage had a picture of 'Tom' Tuby in the centre and his four sons in the corners. One of the films shown was of Jack Johnson preparing for his fight with James J. Jefferies which was to take place on 4th July 1910, in Reno, Nevada. But as war clouds began to gather, so the bioscopes began to disappear off the fair.

Extract from 'A Showman Supreme'

Sing for a Pig

The competitors had to sing one of the popular songs of the period with a live pig in their arms without laughing. The public judged the contest by a show of hands. The one who got the greatest response went home with the pig as a prize. However, the person who had won the previous year was barred to give others a chance.

In the 1930s, Retford was the furthest south that the Tuby family travelled and the appearance of wagons on Spa Common hailed the arrival of the fairground. Young men, some eager for employment, would be ready to help build up the fair. The Half Moon was the favoured place for refreshments as the fair was built on the Market Square. Some of the 'living' wagons were also placed on the Square, carefully arranged in a circle so that the sides of the wagons with windows were all facing inwards and blank sides were facing outwards to give the fairground families some privacy.

Tom Tuby handed down the fairground skills that he had learnt from his father to his son and grandson and it was his grandson, George Rhodes Tuby who sought the help of a carpenter in Retford at the end of the Second World War. Parts of the popular chairoplane ride were in need of repair, but wood was still in short supply and on ration.

George Hurst and Sons, the builders' merchant, operating from premises on Carolgate Bridge, were able to source suitable wood for the repair of the fairground ride. At this time, Spa Common was used by the fairground living wagons when the fair was visiting town. The workshops of Hurst's could easily be accessed from the common as the relief road had not yet been built across a large part of it.

The following extract from 'The Tuby Family History' describes some of the work carried out on the chairoplane ride and shows a wonderful example of specialist fairground terminology.

New legs of hard timber were built, then new swifts were put in where the old ones had suffered from exposure to the weather. New quarterings were fitted and the firm made all new rounding boards for the ride as well as new droppers. And such was the toughness of the wood that George remembers that it was impossible to knock a nail into it. And all this was done on Retford Common.

Tuby Family History

Roger Tuby brings his fairground rides to Retford today. Roger married a Retford girl, Lynne Tomkins who, in fairground language would have been called a 'flattie' as she lived in a house, not a home on wheels. It wasn't easy for Roger and Lynne to see each other before they were married as Roger travelled from town to town with the fairground. Whenever possible, Lynne would catch a bus to wherever the fairground was on and catch a bus home again later. Once she was married, Lynne quickly adapted to life on the move with the fairground, which was a very different life from that in her father's fruit and vegetable shop on Grove Street, which many Retfordians will remember as The Fruit Shop owned by Harry Tomkins in the 1970s and which is still a flower shop today.

A full history of the Tuby Fairground can be read on the Tuby family's website, www.rogertuby.co.uk

Boxing booths like this one were set up on Spa Common.

(National Fairground Archive)

Boxing Booths

Boxing booths were an attraction that often followed the fairgrounds. Retford was host to regular boxing booth showmen, who usually set up their booths on Spa Common.

Bill Durham, a Retford resident, remembers taking part in boxing contests in one of these booths when he was a teenager with no training, just a healthy, strong body and an urgent need to win the cash prize. Trained, experienced boxers travelled with the showmen, and members of the public were invited to try their luck against them in the boxing ring.

Bill Durham bravely volunteered to step up into the ring. He was provided with some boxing gloves, a pair of shorts, a gum shield and soft shoes. The showman's own boxers usually proved to be too strong an opponent for the local lads, but after the fight, the showman would encourage the crowd to throw their loose change into the ring by calling out to them,

'Now come on, ladies and gentlemen, the lad has put up a good fight and kept you all entertained, so please show your appreciation.'

Small coins cascaded into the ring and the 'dobbins' (sometimes known as nobbings) were swept up into a bucket by the local lad. If he won the fight, he would walk away £5 or even £10 pounds better off and would quite possibly be invited by the showman to become one of his travelling boxing team.

Boxing is one of the oldest sports in the world, dating back to the Egyptians of 2000BC and it was one of the first Olympic sports. In England in 1867, the Marquis of Queensbury created the modern-day rules to make the sport more organised. He decided that the regulations would include a number of 3 minute rounds, a count to 10 before disqualification of a floored man, the forbidding of gouging or wrestling and the use of gloves to protect the hands.

Bill Durham greets Eric Brett at a reunion held in July 2007.
Both were members of the boxing club in Retford in the 1950s

In the 1940s and 50s, boxing became a serious and extremely popular sport in Retford, just as it was throughout Britain, and young men like Bill Durham didn't have to wait until the next fairground came to town before they could try their luck in another fight.

Retford Town Hall and the Corn Exchange were both venues for boxing contests, drawing in huge crowds.

Bill remembers taking part in one of several contests in the Town Hall in August, 1946. The Town Hall was full to bursting, with 400 spectators and this is how one of the fights was reported by the Retford Times.

Dobbler Durham (Retford)
George King (Chesterfield)

Durham, who was knocked out in the third round, put up a good show and was beaten by the more experienced ring craft of his opponent. King had the better of the exchanges in the first round, but in the second, Durham countered King's leads to the jaw with a strong right cross followed quickly with a right hook. The Retford man finished the round well.

The third round commenced with King sending his opponent through the ropes but he retaliated swiftly and King was knocked to the boards for a count of eight. Towards the end of the round however, King smashed a hard right to Durham's jaw which ended the fight.

Retford Times 1946

Amateur Boxing Tournament

TOWN HALL, RETFORD
FRIDAY, APRIL 10th, 1953

Officials:
M.C.: MR. GREAVES (Worksop)
NOTTS. A.B.A. OFFICIALS
Prizes presented by Lieut.-Col. G. W. Pick.
Doctors in attendance.

Programme - - - 2d.

PROGRAMME

* F. WOODWARD (Denaby Main)
v.
R. BINT (Newark)

* G. SHERRIDAN (Newark)
(N.A.B. Champion)
v.
J. LAVIN (Doncaster)

§ J. CARDEW (Doncaster)
(All-England Finalist) v.
D. BARNETT, Thorne
(N.C.B. North Eastern Champion)

§ M. G. NEIL (Denaby Main)
(N.E. National Coal Board Champion) v.
S. PEARSON (Doncaster)

† E. BRETT (Retford)
v.
P. KELLY (Sheffield)

§ J. STOCKS (Sheffield
v.
P. ALDRIDGE (Doncaster)

† F. HALLAM (Retford)
(Notts. A.B.A. Finalist) v.
B. SHERRIDAN (Newark)
(Notts. A.B.A. Finalist)

† R. CLARK (Retford)
(Notts. A.B.A. Finalist)
v.
J. MacGARRY (Doncaster)

§ H. CLAY (Sheffield)
v.
E. BAKER (Doncaster)

* D. LIVERSIDE (Retford)
(N.B.C. Champion, 1951) v.
M. MOORE (Sheffield)

† JUNIOR   * INTERMEDIATE   § SENIOR

The First Retford Boxing Club

One of the most influential figures of boxing in Retford in the 1940s was Ken Richardson. As a young boy of 12 years old, Ken set up his own training room in the loft of a barn on Rectory Road, Retford. He was guided and trained by local men such as Sharkey Bell of Ranskill, who was a booth boxer and professional fighter, and also by Dan Anthony, father of Doreen Anthony (a well known teacher of dance in Retford). At the age of 19, Ken was proving to be a formidable opponent in the ring as he became the Light Heavyweight Champion of the Midlands. In 1946, the Retford Times reported that Ken had already won 28 of the 32 contests that he had fought.

The first Boxing Club was held on Rectory Road in the upstairs rooms of this building, known then as 'The Barn'

Ken had many supporters and two of his closest friends at the time were Les Beevers and Harry Tomkins. The friends travelled all over the country to watch Ken fight and Les Beavers remembers a bus of supporters travelling from Retford to White City, London, where Ken had the chance to spar with Freddie Mills (World Light Heavyweight Champion 1948-50) and with Bruce Woodcock (from Doncaster).

Harry Tomkins was a 'second' during contests and was therefore always on hand to give ring-side assistance and it was his job to bind Ken's hands with tape before he put on his boxing gloves. He would also be ready with swabs, water and a bottle of 'Nu-skin' to dab onto cuts. Harry can remember Ken having a knuckle displaced during a fight, but thankfully Dr Livingstone of Retford was able to push it back into position. Home-made remedies for injuries were sometimes made out of anything to hand in the kitchen, such as bacon fat. Harry remembers seeing a joint of ham hanging in the kitchen of Ken's mother's kitchen and a piece of bacon fat was readily applied to a cut or swelling. The general health of these boxers was very good, even though food was on ration. The post-war diet seemed to be ideal for boxers in training, as vegetables were plentiful and often home-grown, with a small amount of meat being eaten each week. The local boxers ate whatever was available and did not follow a particular eating regime and as there were no heavily processed foods, fast foods or easy access to sweets and chocolate, it seems that their normal daily diet was ideal for health and fitness.

Whilst still a young man, Ken opened his training room to other Retford boys, who were keen to train in boxing, such as Frank Pettinger, Derek Liversidge, Eric Brett, Frank Hallam and Ray Clark.

From left to right – Back Row: Ken Richardson, Sammy Hatton, Fred Hartley, Derek Liversidge; Front Row: Frank Hallam and Eric Brett.
(S. Hatton Collection)

Frank Pettinger's training stood him in good stead for his entry into the army where he became a fitness instructor and a referee of boxing matches.

Left: Frank Pettinger in his army days (F. Pettinger).

Below: Frank (right) discusses the old days with Ken Richardson in 2007.

Derek Liversidge aged 12 (P. Laws)

Eric Brett and Derek Liversidge were to prove to be two very successful boxers from the Ken Richardson 'barn'.

Derek started at the club at the age of seven in 1943. Later he trained every night after a day's work at Hurst's the local builders. If he had a contest on a Friday night, he was often allowed to leave work early. Prizes, such as silver fruit bowls, cups, shields and several canteens of cutlery, were plentiful.

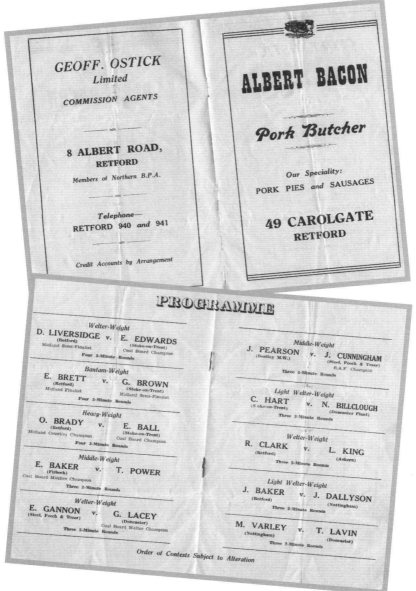

*Programme from a boxing tournament
held in 1956 at the Retford Town Hall
(S. Hatton Collection)*

Eric Brett Appears in the Daily Mirror

Eric Brett, tear-away bantamweight from Retford is the latest sporting personality to join the hula-hoop brigade.

But he's not doing it for fun. The dynamic little boxer has joined the country's latest craze as a serious part of his training routine. And the excess poundage has been sweated off in the right places.

Ten days ago, Brett was 8st. 8lb. Now he is at his best fighting trim of 8st4½lb for next Monday's clash with Irishman Eddie O'Connor at Rotherham

Yesterday, Brett whirled the hoop around in ten minute spells then admitted that it is one of the hardest exercises he has ever tried.

He told me, "It's not as easy as it looks, but it's a fine exercise for getting rid of surplus weight round the hips and waist. O'Connor is a tough customer and I will be at peak fitness when we meet."

ERIC BRETT, the Retford bantamweight, is seen using the hula-hoop to get down his weight for his next fight.

Present

Brett and his manager, Ken Richardson, first saw a hula-hoop on TV, and Eric a keen P.T. enthusiast was taken up with the new craze straight away. Next day a sports outfitter made him a present of a hoop – and that started the whole Richardson stable on the hula routine.

£1000 Offer Refused for Brett's contract

A little bit of real-life drama that might have come straight out of a motion picture about boxing life, was enacted in Eric Brett's dressing room after a recent fight.

Well-known as a boxing manager in the North of England, Mr Jimmy Lumb approached Mr. Ken Richardson, Eric's manager, and said: "Here's a cheque for £1000. It's yours, if you will sign an agreement to say that Eric will fight only under my manager-ship."

Ken took the cheque and held in his hand for a few seconds, but there was no hesitation in his voice as he said: No, Mr. Lumb. My partnership with Eric is not only a business one; it is a friendly one as well. Three times what you offer would not buy off my partnership with Eric," Ken added.

COO! JUST WATCH THAT PUNCH

*Sammy Hatton (trainer) Derek Liversidge, Ray clark, Norman (second name unknown),
Frank Hallam (centre) Eric Brett (with gloves) 1951*
(Parcy Laws)

Boxers Reunited

Almost 60 years have passed since the first Retford Boxing Club began. In July 2007 some of the earliest members were reunited at the annual presentation evening of the current Retford Boxing Club.

For Ken Richardson it was an emotional but very happy occasion as he was reunited with some of the boxers whom he trained. The reunion took place at the Cannon Park football ground on Leverton Road, Retford.

Ken Richardson (right) is re-united with Eric Brett, who was trained by Ken in the 1950s.

A scrapbook containing press cuttings was one of the
attractions at the reunion (S. Hatton Collection)

Eric Brett, Ken Richardson and Betty Liversidge (wife of the late
Derek Liversidge) meet again in July 2007.

Bill Durham and Ken Richardson.

'I was still a teenager when Ken trained me. I remember him telling me that I might not become a great boxer but I would always be able to look after myself. After he had told me that, I won my next contest!'

Bill Durham

When the Film Studios came to Retford

As a young boy of 16, Harry Tomkins found himself signing the Official Secrets Act as he started work as an office boy in a warehouse on Beehive Street. He was unaware at the time that he was playing a small part in a national wartime initiative.

Buildings used by the Air Ministry in World War II, photographed from Albert Road (2007)

Dummies and Decoys

Within four days of the outbreak of the Second World War, a meeting was convened at the Royal Air Force Bomber Command Headquarters, at High Wycombe, on 7th September 1939. The topic for discussion was the feasibility of establishing dummy and decoy airfields to fool the enemy.

Ten days later, the Air Ministry sanctioned the building of two dummy airfields, one for daylight, codenamed K, and one for night, codenamed Q. The person given responsibility for taking charge of the Ministry's decoy programme was Colonel John Turner, a retired RAF officer.

Turner arranged for prototype dummy aircraft to be built. The quotations received from aircraft firms were so high, (they quoted up to £2,000 per dummy), that it was decided to call in the film industry.

In October 1939 Turner went to inspect a dummy bomber – a Wellington – built by Sound City technicians at Shepperton Studios, on the outskirts of London. He was so impressed by the expertise of the Studios' work that he decided to make Sound City his headquarters for the dummy programme. It became known as Colonel Turner's Department and by January 1940, one example of each dummy airfield had been completed. The Air Ministry were impressed with the work and gave Turner the go-ahead to start the construction of K and Q airfields and other decoy sites.

In order to draw the enemy bombers away from our towns and cities, dummy towns, known as Starfish Sites, were set up on open land from one to eight miles distance from the intended target. In daylight, the equipment resembled chicken sheds, etc., but when ignited at night the boilers and fire baskets looked just like bombs exploding, incendiaries burning and buildings on fire – these effects could be made to last a number of hours. Lights were added to Starfish Sites but, on their own sites – known as QL sites, they were designed so that at night they could look like factories, marshalling yards, shipyards, steelworks, etc.. QL sites ingeniously included welding flashes, railway signals, red railway crossing gate lights, tram car electrical flashes and standard lamps.

Secret Workshop on Beehive Street

All over the country, workshops were requisitioned by the Air Ministry so that Sound City could start manufacturing equipment for these sites. An innocent looking building on Beehive Street, just behind Goodbody's Mill, which belonged to E. Hodgson & Sons, was emptied of its horse-drawn hearses and a team working under Squadron Leader Lucas moved in. Working under the Official Secrets Act, employees, such as 16-year-old clerk Harry Tomkins, began the manufacture of decoys.

Due to his good handwriting style, "Young Harry", as he was known, was recruited to log equipment that was returned when it was damaged by bombing or wear. The workshops turned out a whole range of devices. Harry remembers the ingenious "leaky lighting" devices, timber-framed and covered in hessian and plaster, which mimicked open doors and skylights, where someone had carelessly not complied with the blackout regulations, on QL sites.

Of even more interest to a young man who was a member of the local Air Training Corps, was the construction of dummy Boston and Wellington aircraft. Built in sections, using covered timber, these dummies were transported to sites where they were bolted together on top of a trestle base by a small team, who would turn them daily, through at least a right angle, for the rest of their operational life.

Harry Tomkins worked in a first floor office in this building, photographed from Mill Lane in 2007.

Also built at the works were a variety of metal constructions which mimicked the effects of incendiary bombs dropped at night. These devices became more and more technically advanced as the war progressed, and as bombing methods changed. The decoys had to produce fierce fires over a large area, but with differing intensities and for long periods. This was achieved using a combination of oil and water tanks, pipe work, valves and detonators, which gave the impression to enemy airmen, following earlier raids, that a town, city or facility was alight, convincing them to shed their bomb load on what was really open fields manned by a small crew of men who lit the fires.

Dummy Boston Bomber of the type manufactured in Retford
(Public Record Office)

Most spectacular of the decoys was the 'boiling oil fire'. Ten hundredweight (508kg) of coal mixed with creosoted waste was put in a heavy steel trough, over which was placed a steel tray. The device, which measured 62 feet (19m) long, was fed by two separate tanks, of water and fuel. The coal, lit by electric igniters, burned through a cord, thereby opening a valve in the oil supply pipe. 66 gallons (300l) of oil flowed into the still warming steel tray (and over the sides onto the burning coals), a process automatically repeated approximately every 3 minutes. After 20 minutes the tray became hot enough for the oil to burn and vaporize. At this point the water tank released two gallon flushes alternately with those of oil. The resulting mix of cold water and boiling oil produced flames which could reach 40 feet (12m) in the air! With 200 gallons (909l) of water and 480 gallons (2182l) of oil, these fires could burn for 4 hours, producing extreme temperatures and spectacular effects.

Naturally the trays required regular replacements - a record of the old ones were written in Harry Tomkins's ledger.

Harry made use of any off-cuts of wood from the construction work. A keen model aircraft maker, Harry used the wood to make models of his favourite fighters and bombers. His piece de resistance though, was his large scale model of a Lancaster Bomber, made of wood and balloon material, which proudly stood with a real Spitfire fighter on Retford Market Place to promote "Wings for Victory". Harry and his friends in the ATC had to guard the display overnight and they took it in turns to climb into the cockpit of the fighter! Following the display the model bomber was returned to the garden at Harry's parents' house on Bigsby Road, but he had to give it away because local airmen were taking diversions to fly overhead to look at it, much to Mrs Tomkins's consternation!

By the end of the war approximately 630 decoy sites had been built in the United Kingdom, of which, 230 were decoy airfields and 400 were decoy towns, marshalling yards steelworks, foundry and factory complexes. Figures given at the end of the war claimed that the dummy airfields had been bombed 443 times, with the operational aerodromes being bombed 434 times. The decoy towns were bombed about 100 times, drawing some 5% of the bombs intended for towns and cities. Official figures declared that decoy sites saved an estimated 2,500 lives and avoided 3,000 injuries; four civilians were killed through raids on decoy sites. These 1946 figures seem to be on the low side, however, it should be noted that, in most cases, only bombs dropped directly onto sites could be counted as being "dropped on the decoy".

At the age of 17 and a quarter Harry and his pals signed up for the RAF and awaited their call-up papers. Harry went on to work in other jobs to help the war effort, including working in the Ordnance Factory at Ranskill. His call-up papers did eventually come, but by that time the war had ended, and so he was never able to sit in a Spitfire as a fully fledged pilot in wartime.

Harry Tomkins, with his wife Sylvia (left) and Mavis Duke pictured in Harry's Fruit Shop on Grove Street in the 1970s. (H. Tomkins)

Rock n' Roll in Retford

In 1954, the Daily Telegraph reported that boys aged 14 and 15 were arriving at school, wearing their hair in a 'peculiar style' and that the youngsters had paid up to £2 (about £70 today) for the new cut. In Retford, Frank Pettinger and Victor Shaw were already part of the Teddy Boy scene but they were able to get their hair styled in Retford for much less than the teenagers in the cities.

Frank's friends dressed and ready for a night out on the town in 1953. (Frank Pettinger)

The Neo-Edwardian (or Teddy Boy) style arrived from America and swept Britain through the 1950s. Young men adopted the style according to how much they could afford. As Britain gradually gathered its economy together after World War II, young workers found that they had more money to spare to spend on luxuries such as fashion.

It was important to be seen out and about town after spending a large portion of a wage on new clothes and so favourite 'hanging out' places developed such as The Carousel café on Carolgate and the Lilac Domino coffee bar on Grove Street. A coffee or a milkshake could be enjoyed whilst playing favourite rock and roll music on the juke box. The Lilac Domino had a juke box room at the back of the café which could be reached by an alleyway off Grove Street.

The new Teddy Boy style was viewed with caution and suspicion by the older generation. Frank remembers dances at the Town Hall in Retford, (the Harry Clark band being the popular local choice), and a packed ballroom would be moving to traditional waltzes and quick steps, but in a corner of the room, a small group of boys and girls would be jiving and dancing in the new rock and roll style until a steward came along to stop them. The traditional dances such as the waltz, moved in an anti-clockwise direction around the room, but this did not fit in with the style of rock and roll (which used the space on the spot). Teddy Boys and girls could not easily integrate their dancing into the movement around the ballroom, even though it was attempted by many! Small groups of rock and rollers gathered in other spaces of the ballroom but it was seen as outrageous, discourteous and even threatening in the eyes of the organisers. If the ballroom cramped their style, rock and rollers would gather outside. Retford was often buzzing with life on lively evenings in the Market Square where young people gathered to share their interest in the same music and fashion.

Frank described his outfits as,

'Drainpipe trousers, shoes with thick crepe soles and a shirt with a stitched collar or a 'cut away' collar with a 'Slim Jim' or bootlace tie and the jacket was a longer length than usual. My jacket didn't have a velvet collar but some people's did. I bought my clothes from Doncaster or Sheffield, (Winston's in Sheffield). We would travel by train to the City Hall in Sheffield to see rock and roll bands. I had a suit made by Loseby's of Retford, (where Bacon's the Butcher is now). I also had a beige jacket with patch pockets but I didn't like the colour so I took it to Clarks of Retford to have it dyed maroon; it turned out really well.'

Tony Curtis

Teddy Boy hair styles were longer than the usual 'crew cut' of the day and the hair was left to grow up to two and a half inches. Boys and young men would ask for a Tony Curtis cut, named after the film star. Hair was swept from the front to the back on each side of the head and the way that it met at the back gave the style its name of D.A. (duck's arse).

Wired for Sound

Even in the early 1950s, not all homes in Retford had electricity; therefore lighting would be by gas lamp, and electrical items, such as wireless radio players, were not available to all homes. Frank Pettinger's home did not have electricity when he was a teenager in the 1950s but he did not miss out on listening to rock and roll music because his home was connected up to Radio Relay.

The favourite channel at the time, for popular music was Radio Luxemburg. Households paid weekly for this service and the Retford branch operated from premises at the bottom of Carolgate Bridge where the Aldi store is now. The whole town was wired up for music by a series of poles and cables. Because the cables resembled BT telephone cables, many of them have not been removed over the years and therefore home owners may still find old Radio Relay cables still attached to their chimney stacks and outside walls, (if their house was built before 1950).

By the 1960s Radio Relay also included a TV service and the business transferred to a company called Rediffusion which had a branch in the Market Square, Retford. The Rediffusion system was sold to the Maxwell Group and closed down in the late 80s, a victim of better UHF TV aerials and more local relay transmitters. In some towns (such as Hull) the equipment was bought up by different companies and used to distribute satellite channels; in others, like Retford, it was simply turned off.

Claude Green (1898 – 1981)
A multi-talented man remembered.

Claude Green was well known in Retford as a commercial artist and photographer. He was a very active member of the community and as a Boy Scout he became the first King's Scout in Retford and among the first twelve in England. He was also a member of the Ordsall Boys' Cycling Club and worked with the Retford Amateur Operatic Society for more than 30 years.

Claude Green as a fire-fighter (B.Green)

His photographic skills took him to work in London's Fleet Street as a press photographer.

During World War II, he was a member of the National Fire Service, stationed in Mansfield. In the years before his retirement Claude Green was foreman painter for the Retford Borough Council.

He is remembered by many Retfordians for his photography and artistry and also for his entertaining lightning cartoon sketches.

Claude Green sign-writing a vehicle for Jenkins of Retford. Claude also did the sign-writing on vans for Clarks of Retford. (B.Green)

A photographic portrait of Claude's son, Barry, by his father. The cleverly positioned newspaper is a poignant reminder of the pre-wartime setting. (B.Green)

Ephemera from Everyday Life

Over the next few pages are featured items of ephemera that have survived the passage of time. They are things that have escaped the fate of the dustbin by lying hidden in drawers and cupboards for many years, until, at last, they have appeared, unscathed to feature in this book. So here is a collection of everyday items that give us a glimpse of the daily lives of past Retfordians.

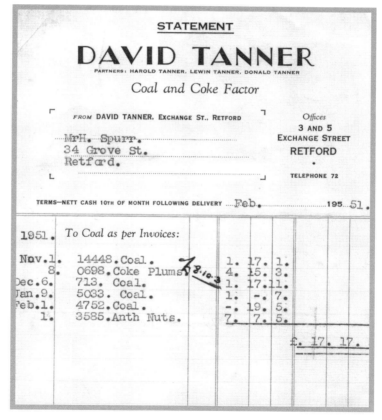

(All receipts courtesy of C. Nangle)

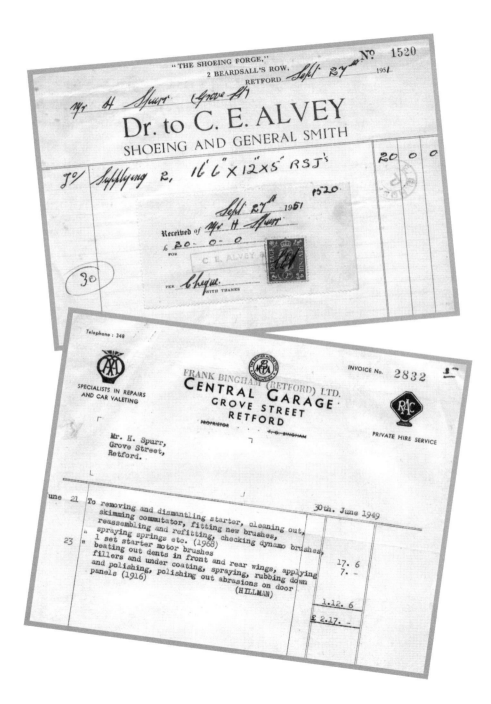

"THE SHOEING FORGE,"
2 BEARDSALL'S ROW,
RETFORD _Sept. 27th_ 195_1_   N⁰ 1520

Mr H Spurr (Grove St)

Dr. to C. E. ALVEY
SHOEING AND GENERAL SMITH

To Supplying 2, 16' 6" x 12" x 5" RSJ's   20 0 0

1520.

Received of Mr H Spurr

Sept 27th 1951

£ 30 - 0 - 0

FOR   C. E. ALVEY

PER _Cheque_
WITH THANKS

30

Telephone : 348

SPECIALISTS IN REPAIRS
AND CAR VALETING

FRANK BINGHAM (RETFORD) LTD.
CENTRAL GARAGE
GROVE STREET
RETFORD

PROPRIETOR   F. C. BINGHAM

INVOICE No.   2832

PRIVATE HIRE SERVICE

Mr. H. Spurr,
Grove Street,
Retford.

une 21	To removing and dismantling starter, cleaning out, skimming commutator, fitting new brushes, reassembling and refitting, checking dynamo brushes, spraying springs etc. (1968)	30th. June 1949		
23	1 set starter motor brushes			
	beating out dents in front and rear wings, applying fillers and under coating, spraying, rubbing down and polishing, polishing out abrasions on door panels (1916) (HILLMAN)		17. 6	
			7. -	
			1.12. 6	
			£ 2.17. -	

70

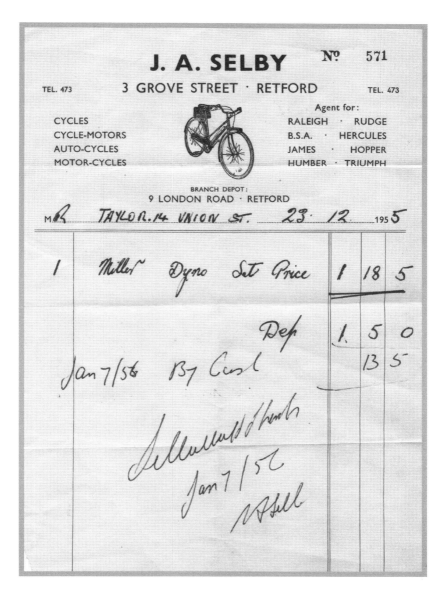

J. A. SELBY   № 571

TEL. 473   **3 GROVE STREET · RETFORD**   TEL. 473

CYCLES
CYCLE-MOTORS
AUTO-CYCLES
MOTOR-CYCLES

Agent for:
RALEIGH · RUDGE
B.S.A. · HERCULES
JAMES · HOPPER
HUMBER · TRIUMPH

BRANCH DEPOT:
9 LONDON ROAD · RETFORD

M R.   TAYLOR. 14 UNION ST.   23 · 12   195 5

1	Miller Dyno Set Price	1	18	5
	Dep	1	5	0
	Jan 7/56 By Cash		13	5

(D Taylor collection)

71

THE MAJESTIC THEATRE RETFORD.

MAJESTIC THEATRE

MAJESTIC THEATRE EXTERIOR.

MAJESTIC INTERIOR

GENERAL MANAGER:
MONTAGUE CASTLEDINE.

TELEPHONE 41

COMMENCING MARCH 23rd, 1953, FOR ONE WEEK

The Traditional Pantomime

"ROBIN HOOD" ON ICE

Produced by Jack Rogers.   Devised by Michael Sullivan.

PROGRAMME: THREEPENCE

"Times" Printing Works, Retford.

PROGRAMME

"ROBIN HOOD" ON ICE

Scene 1 ... ... **The Village of Merridale**

The Villagers ... PEGGY O'FARRELL'S SKATING LADIES

Marjorie Daw ... ... BRENDA NOBLE

Will Scarlet ... ... PATRICIA

Baron Hardup ... ... JACK ROGERS

Robber ... ... CLAUDE ZOLA

Maid Marion ... ... LORETTA WELDON

Dame Trot ... ... MAMIE HOLLAND

Robin Hood ... ... DOORN VAN STEYN

Simple Simon ... ... EDDIE CONNOR

Jack and Jill ... GEORGE REID & ROSEMARY HURDWOOD

Scene 2 ... ... **The Baron's Study**

Baron and Simon: 'Up to their Tricks'; Baron, Will Scarlet, Robber, Dame Trot and Simon: 'H I were not in Pantomime'

Scene 3 ... ... **Winter Snowland**

The Dancing Snowflakes, Jack and Jill, Robber and Robin Hood, Baron Hardup, Snowland Revelry

Scene 4 ... ... **On the Way to the Queen's Castle**

Dame Trot, Baron, Robin Hood, Jack and Jill.

Scene 5 ... ... **In the Queen's Castle**

Swordsmen of the Queen, The Crack Regiment, Simple Simon, Robber, Dame Trot, Baron, Will Scarlet, assisted by Marjorie Daw, Robin Hood: Tribute to the Queen.

INTERVAL

Scene 6 ... ... **Baron's Kitchen**

The Eight Little Maids, Dame Trot, Simple Simon.

Scene 7 ... ... **On the Way to the Nursery**

Robin Hood, Baron, Robber, Maid Marion, Jack and Jill.

Scene 8 ... ... **Circus Dreamland**

The Acromaids ... Peggy O'Farrell's Tumbling Troupe

The Balloon Ballet ... Eddie Connor and Mamie Holland

Clown Auguste ... ... Claude Zola

The Skating Miracle ... ... **Teresa**

Ringmaster ... ... Jack Rogers

Scene 9 ... ... **On the Way to the Woods**

Robbers, Jack and Jill, Simple Simon.

Scene 10 ... ... **A Glade in Sherwood Forest**

Jack and Jill, Little People of the Forest, Robber, Robin Hood

Scene 11 ... ... **The Baron's Parlour**

Simple Simon ... ... Eddie Connor

Dame Trot ... ... Mamie Holland

Scene 12 ... ... **The Palace**

Belles of the Ball, Peggy O'Farrell's Skating Blades, with Robin Hood and Maid Marion (Doorn Van Steyn and Loretta Weldon). Skating Fantasy.

Finale ... ... **Entire Company**

Choreography by Doorn Van Steyn and Jack Rogers.
Special Music written by Francis Baylis. Costumes designed by John.
Ice Engineers: J. Morris, J. Cunningham and C. Mostford
(under the supervision of L. Beresford-Clarke)
Business Manager ... ... Jack Rogers
Stage Manager ... ... Stan Sturges
Wardrobe Mistress ... ... Mrs. D. Clark
Musical Director ... ... Francis Baylis

For CLIFFORD DAVIES ENTERTAINMENTS LTD.
The Entire Production under the direction of MERVAN SULLIVAN

Licensed Bar at all Evening Performances until 10.30 p.m.

Relics from Local Dispensaries

The descriptions of the remedies below reflect the medical wisdom of the first half of the 20th century.

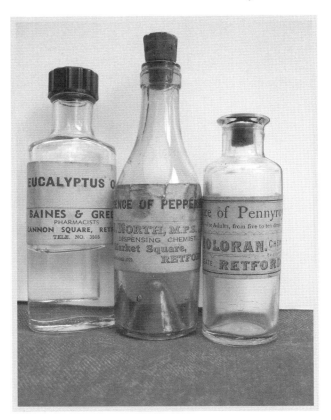

Baines and Green, Cannon Square. Eucalyptus Oil to ease muscular pain and coughs and used as an antiseptic.

F. J. North, Market Square. Essence of Peppermint: used as a remedy for asthma, migraine, bronchitis, a mouthwash and as a remedy for colic.

(F.J. North, the Chemist, was established in 1779).

F. G. Holoran, Carolgate. Essence of Pennyroyal (a species of mint): The name is a corruption of the much older name 'Pulioll-royall' and originally from the Latin name Pulegium-regium. A few drops were taken as a tea for many different ailments such as colds, headaches and menstrual conditions, but a large dose could prove fatal.

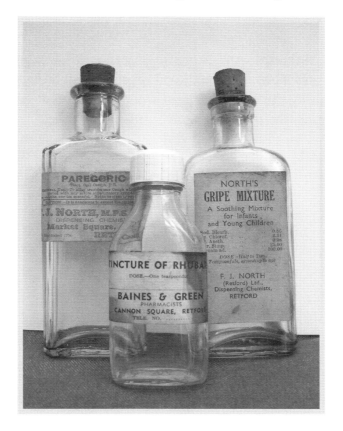

Paregoric: Camphorated tincture of opium mixed with alcohol. Used to control diarrhoea and also used as a cough suppressant.

Tincture of Rhubarb: Used as a laxative and as a tonic for the colon.

Gripe Mixture: An 'old fashioned' herbal remedy that is still available today but without the addition of alcohol. It contains soothing herbs such as dill, fennel and ginger and also sodium bicarbonate to help release trapped wind in infants.

Friar's Balsam: An aromatic liquid with a name that conjures up a possible medieval origin. It contains benzoin and menthol for relieving nasal congestion. Sweet, warm and vanilla-like properties are comforting.

Brandy (for medicinal purposes of course) was bottled by the Crown Hotel, Cannon Square (now the Litten Tree).

(All bottles from the D. Taylor Collection)

Pawnbroker's Sign

Our previous book, 'Down Memory Lane', featured a photograph showing the remains of a pawnbroker's sign attached to the wall of 9 Carolgate. The photograph inspired Roger Jones to suggest to the Retford Civic Society that the sign would be a good restoration project. The Barker family, who formerly ran a grocery and flower business from the premises for many years, kindly funded the project and with the craftsmanship of Roger Jones, the sign can now be seen fully restored.

Before and after restoration in 2007.

A tranquil view of the former Babworth Lake (1960s) (B. Taylor)

The Wire Mill – British Ropes – Bridon Ltd

The wire rope mill on Ollerton Road, Ordsall, Retford was built in 1916 and twenty years later a rope making business was transferred from Dagenham (near London) and added to the site as Retford was considered to be a most suitable area to develop a manufacturing business, it had good rail links, was centrally situated in the country and had a ready workforce (mostly women).

From one World War to the next, the mills were a major source of employment and in some cases, every member of a family worked there. At their peak of productivity in 1950, these two factories employed 900 people with 700 of them being based in the wire mill.

The factories continued to achieve high productivity for the next 20 years and even made it through difficult times in the 1970s when a worldwide scarcity of usable steel forced the companies to work a three-day week. Ironically, at this time there was a boom in the steel trade, but the international demand for raw materials made them difficult to obtain; orders were flooding in but there were no means of fulfilling them.

It was decided that the company would benefit from reorganisation and a change of name was made in 1974. The Round Wire Mill and the Shaped Wire Mill became part of Bridon Wire and The Ropery became a subsidiary of British Ropes and both companies became a subsidiary of Bridon Ltd.. Whatever the names, local people were much more likely to refer to their places of work as 'The Ropes' or the 'Wire Works' but by the beginning of 2003, the company had fallen victim to cheaper manufacturing prices abroad, especially in the East and by the end of the year the factories had closed.

Bridon Limited gates 2007

Betty Liversidge recalls her days at the British Ropes Company.

Betty started work at the British Ropes works on Ollerton Road, Retford as soon as she left school. Her whole family worked there and so it was natural for her to follow suit. The work was dirty, but well paid compared with shop work, Betty earned £2 4 shillings and 10d, which was much more than a shop worker of the same age earning £1 10 shillings.

Blue overalls were worn and workers had to travel to and from the factory in them as there were no changing rooms. No other protective clothing was provided, even the machinery had no safety guards in the 1940s.

Workers would have to watch out for the large 10 inch bobbins that carried the wire thread, as they sometimes shot out of machine with such force that they made holes where they hit the ceiling. Every Friday, the machines were cleaned of the build-up of oil and grease which took about an hour to do; no gloves were worn to protect the hands.

Betty remembers how young people worked hard and played hard, especially when there was a dance to look forward to at the Town Hall. The afternoon shift would be eager to meet the incoming night shift so that they could go straight to town to join in the dancing after a hard day's work.

Betty described the noise in the factory at 'horrendous' and everyone learnt to lip-read as talking above the noise was almost impossible; no ear protection was worn.

The Retford branch of the British Ropes Company mostly made 16mm wire rope which was used by lift makers, ship builders and car manufacturers.

At the age of 18, Betty moved into the office and learnt to type. The large heavy typewriters were designed to make a carbon ink stencil of documents that needed to be copied. Typing errors were almost impossible to correct, so a razor blade was used to scrape away ink from the back of the expensive paper so that it was not wasted.

Despite some uncomfortable working conditions compared with factories today, Betty recalls that the factory had "A lovely, friendly atmosphere. Everyone worked well together and supported each other. We were proud of our work and knew that what we were making was important to the whole country. Placards around the rooms bearing the words 'Their Lives in your Hands', reminded us not to make mistakes."

An aerial view of the wire and rope mills.

(*D. Taylor*)

Clarks of Retford

Clark's Dyeworks began in humble premises on Little Lane.

One of the longest trading companies in Retford was Clark's the Cleaners. In 1798, Hezekiah Clark began work at his own tiny premises (now demolished), on Little Lane off Moorgate. Little Lane has disappeared due to the demolition of buildings to make way for the relief road, Arlington Way. In 1850, the business moved to Grove Street. Charles Clark, who was the grandson of Hezekiah, was quick to embrace modern machinery and the new dyes of the late 19th and early 20th centuries.

In 1892, the laundry department was added, followed by dry cleaning two years later. The Hallcroft Road site was developed in 1904 and gradually, all departments were transferred, as new buildings were added on land previously covered by acres of kidney beans and strawberries.

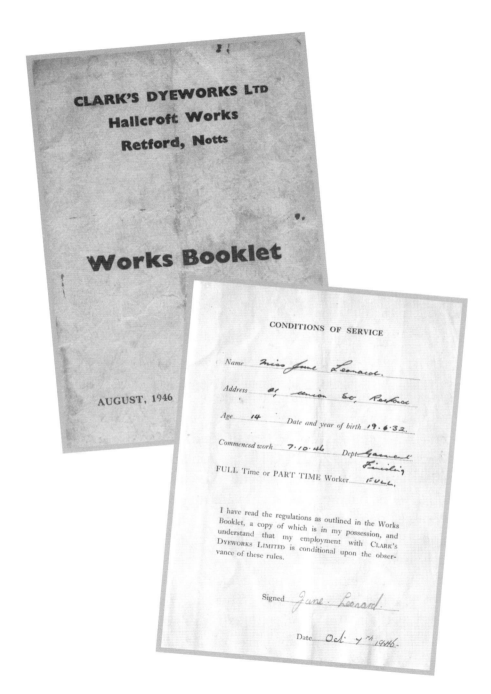

CLARK'S DYEWORKS LTD
Hallcroft Works
Retford, Notts

Works Booklet

AUGUST, 1946

CONDITIONS OF SERVICE

Name *Miss June Leonard.*

Address *01 Union St, Retford*

Age *14*   Date and year of birth *19.6.32.*

Commenced work *7.10.46*   Dept. *Garment Finishing*

FULL Time or PART TIME Worker *FULL.*

I have read the regulations as outlined in the Works Booklet, a copy of which is in my possession, and understand that my employment with CLARK'S DYEWORKS LIMITED is conditional upon the observance of these rules.

Signed *June Leonard.*

Date *Oct. 7th 1946.*

June Footitt (nee Leonard), started work at Clark's as a school leaver in 1946. She was given a copy of the Works Handbook and was asked to sign the back page of the booklet, in acceptance of the rules and regulations within it. Here are extracts from that handbook which was divided into 27 subsections, including rules about smoking, clocking in, and use of the canteen and works welfare.

Safety
One of the first rules to be observed is the correct use of the 'In' and 'Out' gates, All vehicular traffic and cycles must adhere to this regulation. Offenders will be dealt with severely – Three days suspension being enforced.
Employees with cycles must note that it is not in order to walk through the wrong gate with a cycle.

Clocking In
Two minutes latitude is allowed at the start and three minutes at the finish of each working period. This is a privilege granted by the Management to enable workers to collect or dispose of their outdoor clothes and cycles. Any abuse will result in immediate withdrawal of the privileges. An employee clocking in more than two minutes after the official starting time will lose a half-hour's pay.

Medical Examination
All new entrants are signed on as probationers for the first week. During that period they will be required to attend at the Work's First Aid Centre for a minor examination by the factory Medical Adviser. Upon the result of that examination will depend whether the entrant is engaged in regular employment.

Smoking

Owing to the danger of fire and the risk of damage to customers' goods, smoking is strictly prohibited on all premises where work is being sorted, processed, packed or stored. Any person discovered ignoring this rule will be instantly dismissed.

Assisted Meal Scheme

Juveniles up to and including 17 years of age may avail themselves of the assisted meal scheme. Under this scheme younger employees may obtain a full midday meal at the special rate of 6d per day.

Holidays

Employees are entitled to one week's holiday in each year. This, wherever possible, must be taken during the official Work's Holiday Week.

Special Leave

Special leave may be granted to women workers who have husbands or sons in the forces.

Bicycles

All bicycles must be parked in the racks provided. Any employee found tampering with the bicycles will be dealt with severely. Trouble has been caused to employees by the pilfering of such articles as pumps, lamps etc.

Continuation Classes for Juveniles

All new entrants up to and including 17 years of age must take a short course in Citizenship. This class is held each Saturday morning, 11am to 12noon and the hour spent in the class is counted as part of the works week, i.e. with full pay.

June Footitt began her work in the dye room at the age of 14. Her day began at 7.30am and finished at 5.30pm. An hour was allowed for lunch with 10 minute breaks in the morning and afternoon. June remembers that the younger workers (under 21) were not allowed to work overtime and she remembers being pleased when she became old enough to earn extra money by working a long day from 7.30am to 8pm in the evening. Sometimes workers went in on a Saturday too if the department was very busy.

Back Row – Joan Leonard, Jean Gell, Alice Edmonson, Margaret Gell; Front Row – Margaret Smith, Barbara ?, June Footitt

(J. Footitt)

June's first job was to dry and reshape coats. The garments were put onto models (dummies) and held in place with pins that protruded all the way down the dummy. The coat was then pushed onto the model with a brush as the pins would have easily cut bare hands and fingers. Once the coat was in place a lever was pulled to enable hot air to blow through the garment to partially dry it. The next stage involved taking the coat to the stove room where several coats at a time could be dried more thoroughly.

When June first started this job, no protective clothing was provided, so the workers would get dye on their hands and clothes and a trainee would have sore fingers from catching them on the pins that stuck out of the dummy.

June was pleased to be able to progress to the pressing room, (also known as the finishing room). Here she pressed trousers and the quality of the work was inspected by her supervisor, John Hall, who was known as a fair man, but one that would not stand for any slip in standards of production quality or behaviour in the work room.

After 10 years of service, workers were made 'Associate Members' of the Company and were entitled to receive an annual bonus along with the presentation of an enamelled badge, (shown right).

(Badge courtesy of J. Footitt)

Taking a break – on the back row - June Footitt and Margaret Smith
(J.Footitt)

In the pressing room, workers were expected to press at least 32 garments per hour, this made up one unit of work. If workers could achieve a higher output, they would earn a bonus payment. Clothes were pressed at a rate of more than one garment every two minutes and this output was maintained for the full nine hour shift. The only change of routine would be the switch from a morning of pressing trousers to an afternoon of pressing skirts. Monotony was also relieved for about half an hour a day by a radio show called 'Music While You Work' which began in 1940 and ran for the next 27 years in factories all over Britain. June remembers the music being a welcome highlight to the day with young girls singing along to the songs and jigging in front of their pressing machines to upbeat tunes as they kept pace with their work quota. When the music had finished workers would return to their friendly chatter; at least this workroom was not too noisy for that.

Gladys Bussingham worked in the marking department in the late 1960s. Without a good tagging system, garments could easily have gone astray in a huge workplace such as Clarks of Retford. Each piece of clothing, tablecloth or bed sheet was tagged with the customer's reference number. Every single piece was tagged no matter how large or small such as underwear or a man's tie.

The same worker would check the pockets of trousers and coats before they went to be cleaned. All sorts of small objects were found in the pockets and on one occasion a whole wage packet had been left unopened; it was the rule to hand things in to the supervisors.

The task of marking was carried out standing in front of the tagging machine. Gladys remembers the floor being made of cold concrete, so in winter workers would bring a small flat piece of wood to stand on from home, to stop the cold rising up through the thin soles of their shoes. Some of the clothes came into Clark's in a dreadful state and were handled with bare hands until the complaints of the workers brought in the provision of rubber gloves.

Gladys Bussingham (far left) and friends at
Clarks of Retford, in the late 1960s
(G. Bussingham)

Kathleen Freeman (nee Greenside) started working for Clarks at the age of 15 in 1940 and learnt the skill of pressing clothes under the supervision of Winnie Padley; Clem Denman was the foreman. Pleated skirts were steamed by well trained women under the watchful eye of John Hall; Kathleen remembers him as being a strict but fair man.

Like most young women of the day, Kathleen was pleased to be earning her own wage, even though the work was repetitive and involved long hours in a work room where there was no air conditioning, even on the hottest days of the year. Some relief from the summer heat, which was made even less bearable by the hot steamy atmosphere created by the machines, was received when the workers were served a glass of lemon barley water and the factory doors were opened wide to let in any available breeze.

The canteen offered a small selection of filled sandwiches such as egg, ham or cheese and a small variety of cakes such as Madeira cake, known fondly by the workforce as 'roof cake' because it stuck to the roof of the mouth. After a tiring day, which finished at 6pm, Kathleen and her friends walked home (from Hallcroft Road to Thrumpton) as they preferred to save the price of the bus fare.

A promotional gift. The reverse side contains a mirror.
(D. Taylor Collection)

*Clues to the Past - Grove Street, showing the mosaic ''LAUNDRY'
sign and the arched entrance to 'Dyers Court. (2007)*

Grove Street showing the former Clarks Shop. (D. Taylor)

Detail of the buildings formerly used by Clarks of Retford on Grove Street. The alley way leads through to the Chapelgate car park.

The Clarks Magazine

The Clarks Magazine was produced 'for, by and about the employees of the Clarks Group of Companies'. The photographs and extracts that have been included here are from August 1954 and were originally printed by Whartons Ltd. of 29 Grove Street.

It was felt important that the employees had a sense of belonging to the company and so they were kept well informed about changes and innovations that they may benefit from in the future.

The Short Evening Shift

During 1953 and 1954, the company's workload increased to such an extent that they decided to have an extra shift in the evening. This shift was offered to ex-employees who had perhaps left the company a year or so before to raise a family. With the absence of childcare facilities in the 1950s it was extremely difficult for mothers to get part-time work and so, for many, a three hour shift in the evening was ideal at a time when the husband or older children were at home to look after any younger children.

The shift usually ran from 6pm to 9pm, but sometimes an even shorter shift was available such as 7.30 to 9pm, especially in the summer, when a great number of cricket garments came through the laundry. June Footitt took advantage of this opportunity and thought it was a great way for families to earn some extra money.

Clarks reported in the company magazine that they were very pleased with the response from ex-employees and it was a plus for them that they were able to re-employ people

Clarks

MAGAZINE

Dyers since 1798

VOL. 6 No. 7   AUGUST 1954

who were already trained to do the job. Initially, letters were sent out to ex-employees if addresses were known but after a short time people were approaching the Company and offering themselves for work even if they had never worked for Clarks before. The scheme was so successful that the company created a permanent 'Reserve Register'. The register also held names of those who were happy to be contacted for work with only 48 hours notice.

The weather in August 1954 was generally dull and wet and the management at Clarks felt that housewives needed a little extra encouragement to refresh their soft furnishings, as this amusing, descriptive extract from the Clarks Magazine shows.

Eiderdown Recovery

We are now convinced that nobody can tell us when we are going to have weather fit for cooking out-of-doors, and other summer pastimes, but we do know this is the time of year when housewives decide to do something about that terrible old eiderdown on their beds. It will certainly pay to ask every likely-looking prospect if they have thought about having it recovered and persuading them to look at our pattern books and at least to take a hint leaflet away with them. How do you recognise a likely prospect? Any woman with a plain gold ring on the third finger of the left hand!

Clarks Social Club

A Cuddle by the Sea

Clarks regularly organised social events and one such event was a day out to Yarmouth in June 1954, attended by 80 members of the works social club. The bus left Retford just before 7am and arrived in Yarmouth at 12.15pm. The trip was reported in the company magazine as being a delightful day but when it became time for the bus to return home at 7pm, it became apparent that two of the passengers were still missing. The magazine reporter described the couple kindly as 'love birds', however, no names were mentioned.

'Rumour had it that they had eloped, but after a search of all the coaches on the parking ground, we found them as usual cuddled up in a coach bound for somewhere in Yorkshire (Loves Young Dreams). Anyhow, after a bit of coercion they decided to part company (very reluctantly) and we finally got on our way, arriving back home at 2.15am on Sunday, well and truly tired.'

A Works Dance

Tramps' Night Out

The Club Room was also used for a Fancy Dress Dinner and Dance in 1954 and all those attending were asked to dress as tramps.

> The lamb was roasted in fine style and together with the onions, sausages and roasted potatoes, served to a never ending queue of members and friends who thoroughly enjoyed the eatables and the fun around the fire.........
> Those who arrived in anything like a neat condition were immediately thrown into the bushes as had been threatened in the circular announcing the event...after all they had been warned what would happen so had only themselves to blame. Joe, Bill, John, Pat, Ann and Betty were a few who were forced to examine the bushes from ground level but took it all in good part.

And finally.....

At the end of the magazine was a section that listed a few interesting or amazing facts such as:

- **In the 15th century the English were considered to be by far the cleanest in Europe – because most of them had a bath once or twice a month!**
- **Shoes were not always made to fit the left or right foot – until about 1780 they could be worn on either foot.**
- **The "googol" sounds like something childish, but in fact it is a modern mathematical name for the figure 1 followed by 100 noughts.**

Little did they know in 1954 that the word 'googol' would be adapted to the word 'Google' by an internet search engine company, to reflect its mission to organise the immense amount of information available on the World Wide Web.

Bibliography

The Book of Retford James Roffey
(Bookworm of Retford)

Down Memory Lane Angela Meads
(Bookworm of Retford)

Views of Old Retford
North Nottinghamshire from the Air
Life in Wartime Bassetlaw
(Retford Historical and Archaeological Society)

Old Retford David Ottewell *(Stenlake Publishing)*

Images of England – Retford and the Bassetlaw Area
Peter Tuffrey. *(Tempus Publishing)*

Jiri: The Story of Spitfire R7218 Vic Hall
(Country Books)

Retford in Old Picture Postcards Angela Franks and
Greg Franks *(Reflections of a Bygone Age)*

Deception in World War II Charles Cruickshank
(Oxford University Press)

Fields of Deception Colin Dobinson *(Methuen)*

Confettique

Confettiquette

the essential guide to
wedding etiquette

from **confetti.co.uk**
don't get married without us...

First published in 2001
by Octopus Publishing Group,
2–4 Heron Quays,
London E14 4JP
www.conran-octopus.co.uk
Text copyright © 2001 Confetti Network
Book design and layout copyright
© 2001 Conran Octopus Limited
Illustrations copyright © Confetti Network

Publishing Director Lorraine Dickey
Senior Editor Katey Day
Copy-editor Helen Ridge
Creative Director Leslie Harrington
Designer Megan Smith
Jacket Designer Jo Raynsford
Production Director Zoë Fawcett

Thanks also to the staff at Confetti.co.uk,
brides, grooms, guests and Aunt Betti

ISBN 1 84091 228 6
Printed and bound in Spain by Bookprint, S.L, Barcelona

Other books in this series include *The Wedding Planner*;
Speeches; *The Wedding Book of Calm*; *Compatibility*;
Men at Weddings; and *Wedding Readings*.

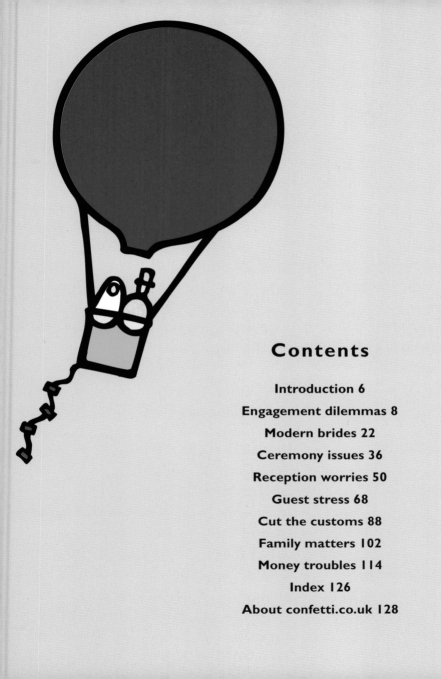

Contents

Confetti.co.uk was founded in 1998 with the express aim of taking the stress out of planning your wedding. With 300,000 couples getting married in the UK each year, and another 52,000 choosing to tie the knot abroad, weddings have never been so popular – or so complicated!

Confetti understands the kinds of questions you're probably asking yourself – and anyone else who'll listen! What actually happens on the day, and who is meant to do what? Are best men and bridesmaids just for show, or do they have a role to play in the planning? You know you need a licence, but what else do you need, and does this mean you can get married just about anywhere?

Or maybe you know about how it's done traditionally but, hey, you want to kick over the traces and stick out your tongue at white dresses and receiving lines. Just how far can you go?

And then there are those you love the most. You want to involve your family in your special day but if you're paying for it yourselves, how much say should they have? Maybe your family situation is a bit delicate. How can you keep all parties happy, while making sure the day is still the best one of your life?

There's also the gift list. As more and more of us set up our homes before marriage, we don't need any more vacuum cleaners or cutlery sets! But how do you let Great Aunt Ada know this without offending her? And is it OK to ask your guests for money?

You'll find all these questions and more answered in this book, but if you have any further questions on confettiquette – the modern etiquette of weddings – and would welcome a sympathetic ear from one who's been there and done it all before, why not ask Aunt Betti? Visit her at the online café at www.confetti.co.uk

Engagement dilemmas

If you're going to take the plunge, the first thing to do is ask someone to step into married life with you. Even at this stage the path to married bliss needs some negotiation. Once you've proposed, so many questions appear! Should you ask her parents? Do you have to do it before you ask her, or can you just ask them afterwards when you know she'll have you? And what if the would-be groom needs a bit of a nudge – can a woman ever propose?

What's the deal with the ring? If you're paying for it, do you have to follow the 'two month rule'? If you're the person wearing it, you've probably dreamt about it – but what if you don't like it?

There are many ways to spread your happy news, from a big party for family and friends to a formal newspaper announcement. But how do you say it exactly? Especially if your family situation isn't mum, dad and 2.4 siblings.

Help! I'm planning to propose to my girlfriend soon, but her father and I don't see eye-to-eye at all. Do I have to follow tradition and ask him for his daughter's hand in marriage?

No, you don't, but it might be a good idea if you do. If you're going to become a part of her family, it's worth starting off married (or engaged) life on the right footing with her folks. Her dad has, presumably, helped bring her up and has been part of moulding her into the amazingly wonderful person she now is. You owe it to him to prove that you deserve her, and it would be great to swallow your pride and humbly ask for his consent. Your girlfriend will be more thrilled than anyone. You could always approach your girlfriend's father after you've asked her, of course.

Should a woman ever propose?

Tradition has it that ladies can propose on 29 February each leap year, a custom that originated several hundred years ago, when the day was considered legally 'invalid'. Conventions were turned on their head and women took advantage of the opportunity to propose. Nowadays, women aren't even waiting for a leap year, and if you think you and your man are set for life, there's no reason why you shouldn't pop the question!

Read our real-life engagement stories for some great examples of girl power at: www.confetti.co.uk/confettiquette/p11

?

Should you propose with a ring?

It's up to you. Historically, the man would get down on bended knee and whip out a few rocks on a band of gold. Nowadays, the couple is more likely to choose the ring together, and it's just as likely to be a ring pull from a can to make do at the crucial moment! You may feel that a proposal isn't a proposal without a ring to hand over, in which case you need to get out there and buy one.

Here are some sneaky ways to work out the size of your girlfriend's third finger:

- Get one of her best gal pals to entice her to try on one of her rings for size and comment on the fit.
- If she's a deep sleeper, wind a length of string once around her ring finger and mark the string with a pen.
- 'Borrow' a ring you know she wears on her ring finger and sneak off to the jewellers. Don't forget that if you do buy a ring ahead of time and it's not the perfect fit, you can always have it altered.

What if he presents you with a ring you wouldn't wear for five minutes, let alone for the rest of your life?

If the man has a ring to offer at the proposal, it will often be a family ring, perhaps one that belonged to his mother or grandmother. In these circumstances, the ring would be difficult to refuse, but you could sensitively broach the subject of perhaps having the stones reset. If he's bought the ring recently, chances are it'll be fairly easy to swap for another. In either scenario, tread carefully!

Prevention is better than cure, however, so why not point him in the direction of our advice on choosing the right ring at: www.confetti.co.uk/confettiquette/p13a

See also our Lad's A–Z of Proposing for more tips at: www.confetti.co.uk/confettiquette/p13b

I can't afford a ring. Should I postpone the engagement?

Let's face it, there's no point in breaking the bank for an engagement ring you both know you can't really afford. Who says you need one anyway? Put the money you would have spent on it into a fund for the down payment on your first house, and promise each other that as soon as the bank balance is looking healthier, you'll invest in a really indulgent piece of jewellery. If you feel strongly that an engagement ring is essential, you could ask your parents for some financial help. They may even have a family ring hidden away, gathering dust and ready to solve all your problems, but try to find out in advance whether it's the type of ring your fiancée would like to wear.

If money's an issue, read our budgeting for your big day feature at: www.confetti.co.uk/confettiquette/p14

Can a guy wear an engagement ring?

Why not? If you wish to show the world that you are engaged by wearing an engagement ring, who is going to stop you? Sure, you might get some odd looks as you simper, 'Look at my engagement ring', but if you're an original kind of person, this shouldn't stand in your way. Traditionally, the bride gives a signet ring to the groom, which is a nice way to mark the occasion.

Want to know what the most stylish grooms are wearing on their hands? Read our millennium grooms feature at: www.confetti.co.uk/confettiquette/p15

Should the bride buy her groom an engagement present?

This is a great idea and a lovely way to celebrate your union – after all, he's just splashed out on that gorgeous ring! Why don't you arrange to go out for dinner and give him your gift then? Alternatively, you could wait until just before the wedding to give him your gift and so celebrate your last few days as fiancé and fiancée. It doesn't have to be a huge present to really mean something. A watch is a popular choice of gift from the bride to her groom but, as with everything else in this wedding business, it's your call.

To find the perfect gift for your husband-to-be, or any other member of the wedding party, visit the gift shop on the confetti shopping channel at: www.confetti.co.uk/confettiquette/p16

My parents are very traditional and would like me to have our engagement announced in a major national paper. What wording should I use?

The announcement is placed in the Court and Social section of national broadsheet newspapers, and the standard format is as follows:

Mr J D Snookesbury   Miss I B Winterbottom
The engagement is announced between Jeremy David,
eldest son of Mr and Mrs Thomas Snookesbury
of Stourbridge, West Midlands,
and Isabella Bertha Winterbottom,
second daughter of Mr and Mrs Rory Winterbottom
of Salterton, Wiltshire.

You could also consider announcing your engagement on the confetti site: www.confetti.co.uk/confettiquette/p17

A less formal way of announcing your engagement would be as follows:

Mr and Mrs Smith of Nottingham are pleased to announce the engagement of their son John, to Jane, third daughter of Mr and Mrs Brown of Curdworth Warwickshire.

If the bride's parents have been divorced the address of each should be given.

Mr and Mrs Smith of Nottingham are pleased to announce the engagement of their son John, to Jane, daughter of Mr Brown of Curdworth, Warwickshire and Mrs Brown, Gotham, Nottingham.

If the bride's parents have been divorced and the bride's mother has re-married the announcement should read:

Mr and Mrs Smith of Nottingham are pleased to announce the engagement of their son John, to Jane, daughter of Mr Brown of Curdworth, Warwickshire and Mrs Red of Gotham, Nottingham.

If the bride's father is dead the announcement should read.

*Mr and Mrs Smith of Nottingham are pleased to
announce the engagement of their son John, to Jane,
daughter of Mrs Brown and the late Mr Brown
of Curdworth Warwickshire.*

If the bride's mother has passed away the announcement
should read:

*Mr and Mrs Smith of Nottingham are pleased to
announce the engagement of their son John, to Jane,
daughter of Mr Brown and the late Mrs Brown
of Curdworth, Warwickshire.*

If the groom's parents are divorced, or if either of his
parents have passed away, corresponding amendments
should be made to their names within the announcement.

Isn't there a rule that the groom's parents should introduce themselves to the bride's parents after the engagement is announced?

It is traditional for the groom's parents to 'call on' the bride's parents soon after their offspring have decided to marry, but it doesn't always happen these days. Generally, the parents will meet at some stage during the engagement (it would, after all, be a mite strange for them to meet at the wedding!), but engagements now are longer and there doesn't seem to be any hurry to make the introductions. It's a nice idea, though, to arrange a get-together as soon as possible after the engagement.

Is it necessary to have an engagement party?

No, not if you don't want to. Chances are, as soon as you've decided to wed, you'll be planning the Big Day flat-out and may not fancy getting your head around organizing ANOTHER party! If the engagement is going to be particularly long, though, why not celebrate the beginning of it with a party? There's no reason why you shouldn't ask friends and family to come round to your place with a bottle, or just meet up in the local pub to celebrate the good news.

Modern brides

Girl Power! You've grown up on a diet of nights out with the girls, *Cosmopolitan* and Gloria Gaynor. So do you have to hide your personality and individuality behind a meringue dress and net curtain veil? And are you going to ask him to obey you? And how do you explain to Aunt Jean that your best mate, the person you know you can count on to arrange that hen night from heaven is, well, a man?

It's completely possible to arrange your fairy tale wedding and still be you through it all. It just takes a little thought and commitment – which is, after all, what it's all about!

Is it up to my bridesmaids to plan the hen night?

The chief bridesmaid generally undertakes the role of planning the hen night. The bride is usually asked whether she has any preference of where she'd like to go and whom she'd like to be there. The rest of the planning and ringing round is then in the hands of the chief bridesmaid (and other attendants, if required).

For the best hen night advice, point your chief bridesmaid in the direction of the confetti website guide to a great night out at: www.confetti.co.uk/confettiquette/p24

Do I have to invite my mother and mother-in-law to the hen night?

This depends on a number of circumstances, including who is responsible for the guest list – is it you or the chief bridesmaid? Are you going to be doing something they will enjoy? Is it practical for them both to get to the venue?

Increasingly, women are having a number of hen parties, partly in response to questions like this one. Nowadays, the bride often finds she has up to three 'last night of freedom' occasions: the traditional-style hen night with work colleagues, a more low-key evening out with female relatives of both families, and a hen day or weekend with her adult bridesmaids and close friends. As more and more brides organize their wedding from a distance, it's often not practical for everyone to get together at one venue on one date, so 'splitting' the party like this not only makes it easier for everyone to take part in the fun, but also increases the fun for the bride!

I've found the most gorgeous wedding dress ever and it's the one I want to buy. The trouble is, it's red. I haven't been married before. Is it OK for me to wear red?

It's a little-known fact that white wedding dresses only became fashionable when Queen Victoria wore one for her wedding. Before that brides simply wore their best dress for the ceremony. The ancient Greeks wore yellow to marry in honour of Hymen, the goddess of marriage, and red is actually the colour often worn at Chinese weddings — it means good luck. So go for it! People will really remember the dress, which is great. One thing though: it might be a good idea to warn your groom that his wife-to-be won't be appearing in radiant white!

?

I'm not at all sure about wearing a veil for my wedding – it's just not me. Must I wear one?

The wearing of a veil is an ancient custom that most brides adhere to. Many say that they wouldn't feel like a bride without a veil! But if the look you have in mind doesn't involve a veil, don't wear one! However, it's always worth trying a few on... you might be surprised at how good it looks! You don't have to wear a veil covering your face; it could be attached behind a tiara. Although most brides do take off their veils for the reception, it isn't necessary. Most veils are secured in the hair with a comb, so they are easy to remove without your entire hairdo collapsing, if that's what you're worried about.

Historically, the bride places the veil over her face before entering the church. The groom then lifts it at the words, 'You may now kiss the bride'. However, some brides do not like this symbolism and lift the veil themselves when they join their groom at the altar, to signify a union of equals.

My bridesmaids are different builds. Can they wear different styles of dresses?

The idea that bridesmaids' dresses are hideously unflattering and expensive and destined never to be worn again has passed into wedding legend. However, recently we've started addressing this issue and looking for solutions that work! One of these, which has become become very fashionable in the last year or so, is selecting either a colour theme or a fabric for the dresses and adapting the style to flatter each individual bridesmaid. This works especially well when the bridesmaids are different ages, and it also means your bridesmaids can select a style they will want to wear at other occasions. This is particularly useful if they are paying for their own outfits.

Must the bride change into a going-away outfit before leaving the reception? I'd rather leave the party in a blaze of glory in the dress I've put so much time into choosing.

If you're going directly from the reception to the honeymoon, changing out of your gown is the sensible thing to do. But you needn't if you're travelling to a hotel for the wedding night. If you do want to change dresses, make sure your going-away outfit is very special and makes you feel great. Don't forget to ask your chief bridesmaid or matron of honour to drop off your outfit (including tights and make-up) at the reception venue. Towards the end of the reception, slip away to change.

If you are planning to leave your reception in a blaze of glory, why not find yourself a novel means of transport, too? Check out: www.confetti.co.uk/confettiquette/p29

Do I have to change my surname and how would I do it?

There is no legal requirement for you to take your husband's surname, but many women do. However, there is a growing number of women who have chosen to keep their maiden names, whether for professional or personal reasons. Your other options are to combine your names to make a double-barrelled surname, or for your husband to take your name.

You can start using your new surname as soon as the ring is on your finger. However, for official purposes, this could cause complications, so you will need to contact all the relevant people (see the list below) who will usually require a copy of your marriage certificate and a covering letter to confirm your wishes to change your name to your husband's. If you don't change your name on your passport, you must continue to buy all travel tickets in your maiden name. This is worth remembering when you leave for your honeymoon and can't wait to use your new name for the first time!

Organizations that need to be notified of your change of name include: DVLA, Passport Agency, insurers (vehicle/home/travel), pension company, building society and/or bank, registrars of any shareholdings, and employer.

Go to www.confetti.co.uk/confettiquette/p30 for legal help with changing your name by deed poll.

Can a bride have male attendants?

Why not? It's not uncommon to have female best men. If your best friend (or friends) is male and likes the idea of performing the role of either best man to the bride or bridal attendant, then you should go for it. But there are some things to consider first. Will anyone who might have been expecting to be a bridal attendant have their nose put out of joint? Will your bride's best man be happy about performing the role, or will he get cold feet on the day? Is he up to organizing the hen night? If it is not commonly known that your closest associate is male, then you may want to start casually spreading the word before the wedding. This will prevent the music being drowned out by the sound of elderly relatives' jaws dropping!

Do I have to carry a bouquet?

Not at all. The role of flowers at a wedding is purely decorative, although the individual flowers do have meanings attributed to them. If you or the groom happen to suffer from hay fever, then it may be a good idea to give flowers, or at least real ones, a miss. Alternatively, carry something striking and exotic but with little pollen, such as bird-of-paradise flowers. Flowers can be very expensive, especially if you have a number of bridesmaids. A lovely alternative is to carry little embroidered bags, that match or highlight your dress, and work just as well at performing the bouquet's primary function, which is to give you something to do with your hands.

What is a bottom drawer, and should I have one?

Having a bottom drawer is a tradition dating from the days when a bride would leave her parents' household only when she got married. The bride and her female relatives would make and buy all kinds of table- and bedlinen, underwear, nightdresses and even baby clothes that would be stored in preparation for her marriage and new home.

Now that many women own their home and furnishings when they get married, this tradition doesn't fulfil the same role, but female friends and relatives may still like to buy you bottom drawer gifts when you announce your engagement.

Do we have to have a gift list?

It's good to remember that people like to buy couples a gift when they get married. It's partly to mark the pleasure everyone feels at such a happy occasion and partly the polite thing to do when you have been invited to a party, in this case the reception. A gift list is a good way of ensuring that your wedding presents are things you actually want or need, as opposed to the fabled five toasters. However, your list does not have to be a catalogue of household items. The confetti wedding gift service at www.confetti.co.uk/giftlist allows you to compile a list of all kinds of activities you would like to experience, from motor racing to having your picture painted. If you feel OK about asking for money, how about opening a Bathroom Fund or Honeymoon Fund bank account for your guests to contribute to? This way they will, in effect, all club together to buy the same big gift! And if you really don't want a gift of any kind, you can suggest that guests make a donation to your favourite charity.

I'm getting married in a church – do I have to wear a traditional wedding dress?

As long as you aren't going to shock the vicar, the verger and the organist, you can wear what you want. Although maybe you could tell the priest in advance so he doesn't expect you to cruise up the aisle in full taffeta sail. Many older brides opt for the stunning suit and hat ensemble, and from here it's only a short step to a trouser suit or short dress. The white trouser suit has been around for so long it's practically a tradition in its own right – remember Bianca Jagger's sleek YSL suit in the early seventies?

Before you make any decisions, it's worth trying on a few examples of every type of wedding outfit. A wedding dress is not the sort of garment you would normally consider when shopping on a Saturday morning, so you might be surprised about what you really look like when you try one on.

If you are planning an informal look, it's a good idea to warn your family and guests, otherwise you might find that some feel overdressed and consequently a little awkward.

Ceremony issues

Deciding you want to get married is easy, but deciding how, when and where is entirely another matter. One of the great concerns for many couples is the marriage ceremony. As this is the part of the wedding that determines whether you are legally married, there are certain rules that have to be adhered to, but that doesn't mean the ceremony can't be fun, unique and memorable!

You can choose from a religious, civil or spiritual ceremony, and for the 40 per cent of couples who opt for a civil wedding, there's a mind-boggling array of register offices and approved premises. Once the venue is decided upon, it's time to address other tricky issues, such as who needs to be present and how to go about writing your own vows. But don't worry! We're here to help you and give you all the information you need to make your day perfect.

I've seen the most gorgeous church ever. Am I entitled to marry in any church I like?

The law concerning which churches you can and can't get married in is rather complex, but basically it boils down to the fact that you must get married in your current parish church, unless you have a very good reason for getting married elsewhere. In this instance, you can apply for a 'special licence', but these are granted only in exceptional circumstances. The number for the Faculty Office, where you can discuss this, is 020 7222 5381.

The other way of dealing with the situation is to attend the church of your choice regularly for six months prior to your wedding. If you let the vicar know this is your intention and you attend services 'regularly' (i.e. two or three times a month), then you'll be entered on the electoral roll and will be entitled to marry there.

For more information, see our religious weddings section:
www.confetti.co.uk/confettiquette/p38a

If you want to get married in a more unusual venue, you might like to consider a humanist wedding:
www.confetti.co.uk/confettiquette/p38b

Can we marry in the evening?

You can get married in a church between 8am and 6pm, every day of the year (including Christmas and Easter if the minister is willing). This is the same for approved premises (civil venues). However, if you are getting married in a register office, the latest you can get married on a week day is 4pm and on a Saturday or Sunday, 1pm. If you plan to marry in Scotland, then you can marry at any time, provided that the minister agrees.

Evening weddings are quite in vogue as lives get busier and busier. However, to ensure you don't have your guests falling asleep as the best man starts his speech at 3am, you may well need to keep events quite tight with reportage photography, short speeches, no receiving line, and a reception at the same location as the ceremony.

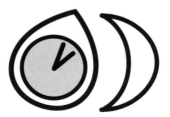

Every venue we like is booked up at weekends for the two months we're considering tying the knot. Is it OK to have a Friday wedding?

Why not? Weekday weddings are a great way of getting the venue you want, and they can work out cheaper, too. However, you should bear in mind that, although you may not have any problems booking the caterers, photographer, cars, etc. on the Friday, getting your guests to attend may be difficult. Assuming that most of your friends/relatives have 'normal' jobs, sneaking away for a Friday wedding could be tricky, and people are often loath to part with precious holiday days. However, if you give guests enough advance warning, these problems can be ironed out. You could even make it an evening wedding, so that your guests need only take the afternoon off if they have far to travel.

For more information on setting the date, go to:
www.confetti.co.uk/confettiquette/p40

?

We have decided to 'opt out' of the traditional white wedding for various reasons, including family pressure to have a ceremony that we're not sure is right for us. But who should we invite to our wedding in Mauritius?

You have two options. You could go it alone, just the two of you, and invite no one. This is certainly the easiest way of proceeding, since you're not deliberately excluding anyone in particular. Your other option is very similar to the standard UK-based reception problem in that you still have to decide whom you wish to be present at your nuptials. But, presumably, you won't be inviting hordes of people, so the problem is somewhat limited.

A friend will be taking the photographs. What are the usual group shots?

The traditional group shots include:

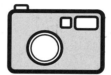

- couple with bride's family
- couple with groom's family
- couple with wedding party
- couple with attendants

The other 'appearances', as they are known, should include:

- groom and best man outside the church/venue
- bride's arrival at the church/venue
- bride and father walking down the aisle/bride entering the venue
- bride and groom at the altar/desk
- exchange of rings
- signing of the register/documentation
- procession out of the church/venue
- group shots outside the church/venue
- arriving at the reception
- cutting the cake

However, a reportage style of photography is very much in vogue at the moment. You might also like to put a disposable camera on each of the tables at the reception. These are on sale at www.confetti.co.uk/confettiquette/p42

Can I get married at home?

In Scotland, the marriage ceremony can take place at any time and in any place that is agreeable to the celebrant who conducts the service. However, in England and Wales, it is not possible to marry at home, unless your home is a registered civil venue or you have a special licence (for instance, if you are bedridden). If you wish to turn your home into an approved premises for civil weddings, certain criteria apply. The venue has to be available for use by anyone wishing to marry, and it has to meet all the local authority requirements in terms of space, fire regulations and the like.

A licence, once granted, is valid for three years. It can take a while to arrange and is subject to a fee, which is set by the local authority. You also need to check with the relevant register office to see if they have staff available to conduct your wedding, and pay the locally set fee for that service.

?

We'd like to hold our wedding ceremony outside. Is this possible?

Provided your celebrant is willing to perform the ceremony, this is very easy to do in Scotland, but it does pose a problem in England and Wales. One way around this is to have two ceremonies: a legal civil ceremony, followed by a humanist ceremony in your location of choice. A humanist ceremony is conducted in the same format as a conventional church ceremony except that the service is all about your love and commitment to each other as a couple, and contains no aspect of religion. You must have a legal ceremony first, however.

?

We'd like to write our own marriage vows. Are there any restrictions?

Most couples consider their vows to be the most important part of their wedding day. However, getting married in a church offers you less freedom to write your own vows than if you're tying the knot in a civil ceremony. For Church of England and Roman Catholic weddings, you are required, by law, to perform a large part of the standard ceremony vows. Usually, the only part you are allowed to change is the 'obey' aspect and to opt for 'respect' rather than 'honour'. This will be at the discretion of your minister, who may help you rewrite certain parts of the vows in line with the religious tradition in which you're marrying.

To personalize the meaning of the ceremony still further, most couples marrying in church like to choose special hymns or readings, or write their own prayers, devoting themselves to each other and asking for God's blessing. However, in civil ceremonies and those of many other faiths, you have more freedom to write your own vows – you simply get the legal part of the ceremony out of the way and then, with the minister's approval, add or subtract lines from the service.

Many couples like to follow the standard marriage vows, simply updating the words with language that's more contemporary. For example:

'I, Lisa, take you, John, to be my husband, my one true partner for life, from this moment forward. For good times and bad, in times of prosperity and poverty, in times of good health, sickness and grief, while we're young and as we grow old, to love, support and respect you, to encourage you for the rest of my life. With God's help, this is my promise to you.'

To signify the fact that you're becoming a married couple, you may want to overlap the lines of your vows as you speak them. For example: Bride: *'I take you, John'* – Groom: *'I take you, Lisa'* – Bride: *'To be my husband...'* Groom: *'To be my wife...'*, and so on.

If you and your groom have a particular passion, such as raising money for refugees, you could incorporate a line into the service promising your combined commitment as husband and wife to the cause. A nice touch is to make guests feel part of your ceremony by adding a line such as: *'Do you, as friends of Lisa and John, promise to encourage and support them in their married lives together?'* The congregation's response would then be: *'We do'*.

If you and/or part of the wedding party come from another country, it's perfectly acceptable to repeat the vows in another language.

If you have children, you'll probably want to involve them in the vows, too. Ask your minister if you can add a line promising that you will both love and cherish your children forever – or whatever is suitable to your circumstances.

If you don't hold any traditional beliefs about weddings or are not religious, you could opt for a humanist ceremony. Then you'll be able to write your own vows from scratch, reflecting your love for each other, for any children you have and for any other facet of your relationship.

I would like to arrange a surprise wedding for my fiancé(e). Is that possible?

It can't be a complete surprise. Before two people get married, they have to give notice, even in a civil venue, and in a church both parties are required to meet the minister in advance, which would certainly spoil the surprise! The terms of giving notice include the couple being resident in the area in which they intend to marry for seven days before they can apply for a marriage licence on the eighth day (but see also page 38). You then have to wait a further 15 days for the licence, and you have up to one year in which to use it. You can, however, surprise your partner with the date, venue and guests.

How many witnesses is it necessary to have at our wedding?

Each wedding must be attended and attested to in writing by two witnesses. These can be anyone who is willing to perform this service, including passers-by off the street! However, they are more usually the parents of the couple or the best man and chief bridesmaid. Your children can also be witnesses, but it is preferable though that the witnesses are of an age to understand what is going on, and this usually means in their early teens upwards.

Reception worries

Who sits next to Great Uncle John? When do we cut the cake? It's hard to know what the 'right' things are when planning your reception and, in any case, do you want to do the 'right' thing? Do you want to follow tradition but add a twist of your own? This is your big day, and there are no rules that you have to follow when planning your reception – only to make sure that it's what you both really want. You don't have to order a three-tier traditional wedding cake if you and your partner like the idea of having something a bit more fun. (What about a huge pile of chocolate profiteroles? Or individual sponge cakes?) You don't have to have a top table if you think that the parents will explode at the thought of sitting next to each other. There's not even a rule to say that you have to feed your guests with a three-course meal! So, stay calm and start planning the celebration to end all celebrations!

What is a receiving line, and who should be in it?

This a line formed by you, your spouse and often both sets of parents so that you can all be properly introduced, in turn, to everyone at the reception and each guest is made welcome. It can take place either as people arrive at the venue or as they make their way into the dining room if drinks are being served first. It is becoming increasingly popular for a master of ceremonies to announce each guest as they enter the room, so everyone in the receiving line knows who they are about to speak to.

Some couples prefer to greet their guests on their own, but if parents are in the receiving line, it is advisable to go through the guest list with them before the day so that everyone is acquainted with the guests' names.

Traditionally, the order of people in the line is as follows: bride's mother, bride's father, groom's mother, groom's father, bride, groom. The bride's mother and father come first in the line, as traditionally they are the hosts, although this is not always the case nowadays.

If you have lots of guests attending the reception, it is a good idea to keep the receiving line as short as possible. Having just the two of you greeting guests will prevent long queues.

? Do we have to provide a sit-down meal for our guests or is it OK to have a buffet?

There is no rule to say that the meal you serve has to be a hot one. You may prefer to give your guests a simple cold buffet. This could comprise salads, a selection of cold meats, a large salmon, bread and dressings, followed by fresh fruit, gateaux and pastries, cheese and biscuits (see also page 59).

My fiancé and I would like to have a themed wedding. Is this acceptable?

Many people choose a theme for their weddings based on their favourite colour, or flowers, or location, so it's just a small step to a more flamboyant theme. If you prepare your guests well in advance so they know they will be expected to dress up/bring their favourite teddy bear/dance the Charleston, they'll love it as much as you will.

The key with any theme is to carry it through from the invitations to the thank you cards, in order that everyone recognizes it as such. So if, for example, you were to take the 1970s as your theme, you could send out psychedelic invitations asking your guests to come in costume, have an Elvis impersonator to sing at your reception and then dance the night away to a medley of golden oldies.

If you'd like to introduce a theme to your wedding, then spend some time thinking about whether your guests will enjoy it as much as you. Try to decide on something that will be as enjoyable for your grandmother as for your friends. It's a tall order, but it can be done.

?

How do we make the evening guests feel as welcome as those who've been with us all day?

If you've invited a number of your friends to the evening part of your reception, then it's important to make sure that they have a good time. With so much to arrange for the ceremony and the main part of the reception, it's all too easy to assume that they will simply join in with the party. But there are a few things that you can do to ensure that the new guests feel welcome and relaxed.

First of all, work out what time you expect the meal and speeches to end and ask your evening guests to arrive no earlier than 45 minutes later. This will allow time to clear away the meal and set up the music, if you're having any. Encourage your day guests to move from their seats and mingle, perhaps moving to a new drinking and dancing area. If space is limited, arrange for the main tables to be moved to the side. This will make it easier for your evening guests to blend seamlessly into the party.

Another idea is to wait until your second wave of guests have arrived before you cut the cake. This is a simple way to include your evening guests in the more traditional part of your reception.

Do we have to have a seating plan?

Although it is traditional to have a seating plan, and some of your older guests may be expecting one, it is not essential. It really all depends on the style of meal you wish to serve. If you are having seated dining with table service, a plan does prevent confusion if you indicate to guests where you wish them to sit. Some guests may expect your close relatives to be seated on or near the top table, but don't worry if this is not what you really want. The order of seating for a top table is, from left to right as you face the table: chief bridesmaid, groom's father, bride's mother, groom, bride, bride's father, groom's mother, best man.

If you do opt for a seating plan, consider having more than one on display, so that there won't be a huge scrum of people trying to find out where they're supposed to be sitting. Alternatively, you could be a little more creative. For example, hand each guest a bag of sugared almonds with a card attached telling them which seat they have been allocated.

If you are having a very informal, picnic-style buffet, then scatter tables and chairs around the room and let your guests decide where they sit. But make sure you let everybody know that they can sit wherever they like.

For some online table planning help, go to:
www.confetti.co.uk/confettiquette/p56

When do we cut the cake? And can the cake double as dessert?

Cutting the cake is usually done after the speeches (after the meal). However, if you wish to eat it as a dessert, it will need to be cut as soon as possible. If you want your guests to witness this, the best time would be as soon as everyone is settled at the reception, when the welcome drinks are handed out. This way you allow your caterers enough time to prepare the cake as dessert.

You may find that a number of your older guests will like to take their wedding cake home, so it might be nice to hold some of it back. It's also traditional to send a piece of cake to guests who are unable to attend, to let them know you are thinking of them.

If you are going to use your cake as dessert, why not consider an alternative to traditional fruitcake, such as chocolate cake or croquembouche?

Should we invite the vicar to the reception?

You should certainly invite the vicar to the reception – this is standard etiquette. If the vicar has a wife/partner, he/she should also be invited.

Although your vicar is used to going to lots of weddings where they know very few people, it is a nice gesture to introduce him or her to some friends or relatives, especially if you know they may have something in common. It would also be considerate to give him or her an estimated timetable of the day, so if he or she has to disappear off, they know when they can do it politely and comfortably.

My fiancé and I are vegetarian and would like to have an all-vegetarian meal at the reception. Is this acceptable?

Why ever not? If you're not keen on serving meat to your guests, there's absolutely no reason to do so. However, if you choose to go completely vegetarian, think carefully about what to serve. There are always one or two die-hard carnivores around who will be dying to bash an all-vegi menu, and what fun it would be to pleasantly surprise them!

Is it OK to have a 'dry' wedding reception, and should we let our guests know in advance?

It is fine to have any kind of reception you feel comfortable with. The issue of serving alcohol or not may affect your guests' practical decisions, such as whether they drive to your wedding or leave the car at home and stay overnight, so it is a good idea to let them know in advance that the reception will be 'dry'. If you think that most of your guests will be surprised that alcohol will not be served, then advance warning may prevent the lack of alcohol being the main topic of conversation at your reception!

Do we need a toastmaster, and what would he or she do during the reception?

You may choose to employ a professional toastmaster (or master of ceremonies) to conduct the entire reception, introducing the bride and groom formally as they enter the reception as well as introducing the speeches. He or she would also introduce each event of the celebrations, such as the receiving line, the serving of the meal, the cutting of the cake, and the first dance. In the absence of a toastmaster, the best man is called upon to introduce the speeches.

What is the order of the speeches and should the bride ever make a speech ?

The formal order of speakers is:
- Father of the bride (or a close family friend)
- The groom
- The best man

But if the bride, chief bridesmaid or guests want to speak, then that's great, too!

It is important that the speeches don't go on for too long. If the groom, the father of the bride, the best man and the bride all make speeches, it can turn into a bit of a marathon for the guests. If, as the bride, you really want to speak, then it's a nice touch, but the entire speech section of the day should be kept to around 20 minutes, 25 minutes maximum.

As my father won't be present at the reception, can my mother speak instead?

Of course she can. You can ask anyone you like to make a formal speech. If your mother has given you away she could make the traditional Father of the Bride speech, which is the first in the order. If someone else is making this speech, or you are doing away with it, she could speak either after this or at the end of the speeches.

For more details on who should say what and thank whom in their speeches, as well as loads of ideas for more unusual twists, see the confetti.co.uk book *Speeches*.

When should the bride throw the bouquet?

Traditionally, the bouquet is thrown just as the bride leaves the reception. All unmarried females are asked to gather round the bride, who then throws her bouquet over her shoulder. The person who catches it is said to be the next to marry. If you don't want your male guests to miss out on all the fun, you could adopt the American tradition where the groom removes his bride's garter and throws it over his shoulder to the waiting single men. Whoever catches it will be the next man to marry.

How do we begin the dancing?

When the band kicks in, the first on the dance floor should, by rights, be the newlyweds. Lots of couples plan their first dance as man and wife very carefully and choose a song that means something special to them. Then the rest of the party joins in, with, according to tradition, the groom dancing with his new mother-in-law and the bride with her father. After that the bride dances with her father-in-law and the groom with his mother. Finally, the groom and the chief bridesmaid take to the floor, while the bride and best man dance. If you're not a great mover, or just feel uncomfortable about dancing in public, open the dance floor to everyone as soon as the music begins.

? **We're paying a lot of money for this wedding. Do we have to 'go away' just as the fun begins?**

Of course not. You'll probably want to party till you drop – but be careful about drinking too much! However, some of your older guests will consider it polite to stay to see you off, so do let them know beforehand that you are planning to dance the night away and that they don't have to stay!

A lovely farewell when you (finally) leave the reception is for all the guests who've still got the stamina to create a 'tunnel' of arched hands for you to pass under. This way you get to say goodbye to all your guests – a reverse receiving line!

I can plan everything, but I can't control the weather. How can I ensure my guests' comfort?

Most weddings take place during the summer months in order to take advantage of the sunny weather, but even in high summer you can still be caught out by bad weather. To ensure that rain doesn't put a dampener on your day, there are a few things you can arrange, just in case.

First, ask each of your ushers to bring their biggest umbrella. Then, if the skies open when you and your guests are moving from the wedding to the reception, the ushers can meet each car and escort everyone through the rain.

If your reception will take place in a marquee, then you could arrange for heaters, in case the temperature drops to an uncomfortable level.

Similarly, if temperatures look like they could rise to boiling point, think about setting up sun umbrellas and perhaps some fans. Don't forget that your guests will probably drink more in the heat, so you may well need to order extra water and ice.

You can check your wedding day weather forecast by visiting the met office website at www.meto.gov.uk

Guest stress

Just who do you put on your guest list?
Will anyone ever speak to you again if you tell them
you don't want children at the wedding? How do you
invite friends to the evening party, but not to the
meal? No one wants to upset anyone else, least of
all when you're planning a celebration as wonderful
as a wedding. But the size of your venue or cost of
your wedding may create constraints that you have
to work within. Once you've sent out the invitations
(when should that happen?), what do you do if the
replies don't start flooding in immediately? First
things first – you don't panic! Instead, take a deep
breath. We're here to help. By the end of this chapter
you'll end up with the guest list you really want.

We're getting married in 18 months' time. When should we send out the invitations?

You should send out invitations as soon as you have set the date, found the reception venue and decided on the guest list. Theoretically, invitations should be received six weeks before the wedding, allowing guests plenty of time to RSVP. With summer weddings, it's probably wise to give guests a little more notice as the summer months are when people tend to get double booked or go away on holiday. It is fine to send out your invitations two or three months before the celebrations – some invitations go out as early as a year in advance – but if the ceremony is being arranged in a hurry, it may not be possible to give everyone very much notice. The later you send your invitations, the more you need to be prepared for people being unable to attend.

The American custom of 'save the date' cards is a great idea. These can go out as soon as a date and venue are decided upon, and can say something as simple as: 'Sabrina and Paul will be getting married on such and such a date. Please save the date so you can share our day with us!' To see some examples, go to www.confetti.co.uk/confettiquette/p70

We would like to send out formal invitations. What is the correct wording?

The wording for a formal invitation may vary according to personal preference but, whatever the format, it should always state the following:

- names of the bride's parents or other hosts
- first name of the bride (if her parents are the hosts, full name if not)
- first name and surname of the bridegroom and his title (Mr/Lieutenant/Sir, etc.)
- where the ceremony is taking place
- date, month and year of the wedding ceremony
- time of the ceremony
- location of the wedding reception
- address to which guests should reply

Invitations always go out from the wedding hosts – usually the bride's parents. The wording changes if parents are divorced or if the bride and groom are hosting the event themselves. The usual wording for a traditional invitation is:

Mr and Mrs James Jones request the pleasure of your company (or: request the honour of your presence) at the marriage of their daughter Susan to Mr Neil Wood at St Mary's Church, Milton, on (date, month, year), *at* (time), *and afterwards at* (reception location). *RSVP* (hosts' address).

My father passed away last year. What should we write on the wedding invitations?

The wording can be adapted to accommodate a change of circumstances. For example:

Mrs Pamela Jones requests the pleasure of your company
at the marriage of her daughter Susan to Mr Neil Wood
at St Mary's Church, Milton, on (date, month, year), at (time),
and afterwards at (reception location). RSVP (host's address)

My parents are divorced. How should the invitations be worded?

There are several ways of approaching this situation. The most simple is to include your parents' full names, which underlines that they are individuals, rather than a married unit. For example:

Mr James Jones and Mrs Pamela Jones request the pleasure of your company at the marriage of their daughter Susan to Mr Neil Wood at St Mary's Church, Milton, on (date, month, year), at (time), and afterwards at (reception location). RSVP (one host's address).

If your parents are divorced and your mother has remarried, then the invitations should simply read:

Mr James Jones and Mrs Pamela Matthews request the pleasure of your company at the marriage of their daughter Susan to Mr Neil Wood at St Mary's Church, Milton, on (date, month, year), at (time), and afterwards at (reception location). RSVP (one host's address).

Alternative wording examples

When the wedding is hosted by:

Both sets of parents

Mr & Mrs Wakefield and Mr & Mrs Austin request the pleasure of your company at the marriage of Laura Elizabeth Wakefield to Adam John Austin on (date, month, year), at (time), at St George's Church, Barton-in-Fabis, Nottingham.

The bride and groom

Ms Laura Elizabeth Wakefield and Mr Adam John Austin request the pleasure of your company at their marriage on (date, month, year), at (time), at St George's Church, Barton-in-Fabis, Nottingham.

The bride and groom with both sets of parents

Mr & Mrs Wakefield and their daughter Laura Elizabeth, together with Mr & Mrs Austin and their son Adam John, request the honour of your presence at the wedding of Laura Elizabeth and Adam John on (date, month, year), at (time), at St George's Church, Barton-in-Fabis, Nottingham.

A single parent

Mr Wakefield requests the pleasure of your company at the marriage of his daughter Laura Elizabeth to Adam John Austin on (date, month, year), at (time), at St George's Church, Barton-in-Fabis, Nottingham.

A divorced parent with their spouse

Jane & Tom Brown request the pleasure of your company at the marriage of Jane Brown's daughter Laura Elizabeth Wakefield to Adam John Austin, son of Mr & Mrs Austin, on (date, month, year), at (time), at St George's Church, Barton-in-Fabis, Nottingham.

Someone other than the bride's parents

If the hosts of the wedding are neither the bride's nor the groom's parents but another relation, you should omit the word daughter/son and add the host's relationship.

- grandparents = granddaughter/grandson
- aunt and uncle = niece/nephew
- godparents = goddaughter/godson
- foster parents = foster daughter/foster son
- brother = sister/brother
- sister = sister/brother

Not all of my family get along. How do I ensure they keep the peace?

The million-dollar question! First, you should sit down with them beforehand, individually and jointly, and express your concerns. Ask them what they think can be done to avoid conflict. It may be as easy as making sure they are seated separately at the reception, or keeping the speeches short so Great Uncle Alex doesn't get the chance to drink too much! Explain that you really want everyone to be there to share your special day with you, and you don't want to feel unable to invite people to your wedding. Ask them to put aside their feelings for the day. If you are still worried, brief a close friend or two in advance, so they can keep an eye out for any conflict that might be brewing.

We'd like our guests to conform to a dress code. How do we say this on the invitation?

It is not only acceptable but also welcome to guests to have the dress code indicated on the invitation (usually in the bottom right-hand corner). This may be suggested in a number of ways, such as the succinct 'Black Tie', which essentially means tuxedos for gentlemen, and evening dresses for ladies, or 'White Tie', which means tails for men, and ball- or full-length gowns for women. 'Morning Dress' and 'Lounge Suit' are terms not used very often these days and are best avoided if you don't want calls from anxious or confused guests! However, if you wish your dress code to be something out of the ordinary, you can always say 'Fancy Dress', 'Purple Attire', 'Denim and Diamonds' or whatever takes your fancy!

Should we enclose the wedding list when we send out the invitations?

Traditional etiquette has it that the couple should wait until they are asked before they tell guests where their wedding list is being held. But if your guests are busy people, they would probably appreciate knowing where you have placed your list. If you really dislike the idea of including the list with the invitations, then send them out separately afterwards. However, some gift list services provide attractive little list cards that can be sent out with the invitations.

A subtle way of pointing your guests towards your gift list is to include details of it on a personalized wedding web page. You can set one of these up through confetti.co.uk.

For details of the confetti.co.uk gift list service, go to:
www.confetti.co.uk/giftlist

What is the etiquette for notifying people that our wedding is for adults only? We don't want to cause offence but we just don't want the kind of wedding that involves children.

If children are invited, this can be made clear by including their names on their parents' invitation. Parents should assume that the invitation is for them alone if their children's names are not specified, but to make things crystal clear, it might be tactful to enclose a short note to parents that says something like: 'Much as we would like to invite all the children of our friends, it is only possible to accommodate the children of close family,' or 'We are sorry we are unable to accommodate children.'

If you have your reception at a hotel, there may be a smaller room in which children can be looked after. This way, you won't offend those with children and you won't have kids under your feet all day. Let parents know up front if you have made special arrangements for their children: 'We have arranged child-minding facilities for the duration of the service and/or reception.'

I'm close to a couple of work colleagues and would like to invite them. However, I don't really want to invite everyone at work. How can I do this without upsetting anyone?

Inviting colleagues can be tricky, and it's easy to cause offence by inviting some and not others. You could just try the secretive approach and ask your invitee to keep it quiet, but if you're found out, this can make the situation worse. Alternatively, you could just invite those in your department or who work on your floor, or go for the all-or-nothing approach – the more the merrier or no one at all.

How do we invite friends to the evening party but not to the meal?

There are a number of ways in which you can handle this tricky situation with charm and style. The first is to contact your friends and relatives individually, explaining that you are having a small wedding in Mauritius/Hackney Register Office. What is your reason for wanting to limit the guest list? Many people invite only close friends and relatives to the service and first part of the reception, and then invite more friends to the later part of the day. A note could be included with the invitation as follows:

It is with regret that Sarah & Josh are unable to invite everyone they would like to join them all day in their wedding celebrations, due to number and cost restrictions. It is their hope that you will understand the reasons for this and that you will accept their invitation to the evening celebrations.

Or, less formally:

Please join Sarah and Josh to celebrate with them after their wedding ceremony on June 17th. Drinks and dancing from 7pm.

If you are sending out invitations for the wedding reception or evening reception only, these can take the same form as any usual party invitation.

Family and close friends are usually addressed informally as, say, Alan and Anne; otherwise guests are given their usual prefixes such as Mr and Mrs, Captain and Mrs, etc.

?

It's two weeks to go and some guests still haven't replied! What do we do?

Don't worry. Generally, people who can't make it to the wedding reply first because they know they can't come and want to let you know ASAP. You'll probably find that all your friends who haven't yet replied can come but assume you already know that, or they just haven't got round to sharing the knowledge with you that they will be there! However, you will want to know the numbers for the day, so a few phone calls are in order. This could be a good task to divide up between your parents and yourselves; the best man and chief bridesmaid would probably lend a helping hand as well.

Can we ask our guests to pay for their own drinks at the reception?

Certainly you can, and in a recent survey on *www.confetti.co.uk*, 85 per cent of couples said they thought it was perfectly acceptable to do so. However, it is always good manners to warn people that this is the case in advance – women, in particular, may not be carrying money unless they know they have to. You can slip a note in with the invitation or wedding information pack if you are sending one out, saying something like:

There will be a full cash bar from 7.30pm. Please note, there are no cash point machines in Lower Nettlingfold. Cigarettes are available from the Fox and Chickens pub next door.

What is a wedding information pack, and what should we include in it?

Wedding information packs have become a necessity nowadays as couples celebrate their weddings in assorted distant locations. The pack is basically a few notes to give your guests the additional information they need about the wedding, such as maps and details of local accommodation.

Some couples include their wedding pack with their invitations, while others send them out later to those people who request them. If you prefer this option, then add a note on the invitations asking your guests to say if they would like a copy of the wedding pack when they RSVP.

The basic information you should include should be details of how to get to the wedding and reception, including train times; taxi telephone numbers and parking availability; convenient accommodation; restaurants; and tourist information for those who plan to make a bit of a trip of it.

This is also your chance to let people know more about the wedding, if you are going to include anything unusual, and of course, details of where you are holding your wedding list.

If some of your guests are online, you can create your own wedding web page and include all the wedding details. To find out how to do this, go to www.confettiquette/p86

Some of my guests are coming a long way. How can I make this easier for them?

First off, make sure your guests have the name and phone number of someone you have appointed as a 'guest liaison' – someone who can be contacted with questions and queries, because you won't have time!

If most of your out-of-town guests are arriving the evening before the wedding, suggest a time they can meet in a hotel bar and get acquainted before the wedding. This is particularly nice if you are having a rehearsal dinner with your wedding party and can't spend time with your guests.

If your guests aren't familiar with the traditions of the wedding you are having, let them know beforehand what the layout of the day might be, as this will enable them to relax and enjoy the day with you more.

Cut the customs

**Is it really imperative that someone gives
you away?** Is Flora Jane going to make a good best
man? Just when you think you finally know what you
want, you realize that everyone has an opinion on
your big day and is eager to tell you about some
great tradition that's been in the family for years.
Worse, they assume that you'll be following it! If you
want a wedding that is for you and about you and
disregards all those traditions and customs you'd
really prefer to ignore, this chapter tells you how to
go about it. This is the time to let both of your
personalities shine through. You never know, you
might even end up creating some of your own
customs that you can pass on!

Can we have a joint hen/stag night?

Traditionally, hen and stag nights marked a farewell to your same-sex group of friends before the start of married life, and it still heralds a goodbye to the single life. Therefore, most people tend to view them as single-sex events, although, to an extent, this depends entirely on what you want to do — at the risk of stereotyping, the bride may be happier spending a weekend at a health spa with a bunch of girlfriends rather than with a mixed group. However, some people do combine the two events into a big party. If most of your friends know each other, then this has its advantages, but there are also practical considerations, such as the matter of babysitters if your friends have children.

?

What is a bridal shower, and how do I go about giving one?

Wedding showers are really an American thing, but there's no reason not to give one over here. A bridal shower should take place after the engagement party (if there is one) and several weeks/months before the actual wedding. In America, the maid of honour usually arranges the event, which can be held anywhere, from the bride's house to a beach! It's a women-only thing, and all the bride's closest friends and relatives go, along with the groom's close womenfolk, too. Guests turn up with gifts for the bride – traditionally, essential items for setting up a new home. These days, though, many shower gifts are more indulgent, for example, a spa voucher or a sexy item of underwear. The occasion has become quite lavish in the US, and in many cases the shower actually gives the wedding reception a run for its money! But a shower can be as extravagant or as low key as you want.

What is a rehearsal dinner, and must we give one?

A rehearsal dinner is another American tradition and one that's not really caught on over here yet. The idea is that the evening before the wedding everyone directly involved in the celebrations gets together for a run-through at the ceremony venue, and then has a big knees-up to celebrate. The tradition is that the dinner is hosted and paid for by the groom's parents. It's a nice way to thank those people (including parents) who have been supportive and helpful during the engagement. In the UK, ceremony rehearsals tend to take place several days before the wedding, but if you do decide to go ahead with a rehearsal dinner, you should just invite those who will be involved in the ceremony – that is, the best man, both sets of parents, ushers, bridesmaids (and their parents if the bridesmaids are under the age of 16), and remaining close family.

For more information about what happens in the run-up to the wedding, visit our engagement section:
www.confetti.co.uk/confettiquette/p92

?

Can the groom have a female best man? Or, possibly, even two?

The best man's role is, briefly, to be supportive of the groom in the run-up to the wedding, organize a stag night, marshal the ushers on the day, make sure the rings make it to the church and give the best man's speech. The right man for the job could very well be a woman, but just make sure the bride is comfortable with the idea! Many grooms split the best man's duties between two friends or relatives: one to take on the pre-wedding duties, including organizing the stag night, and the other to perform the role on the day. Having two best men at the actual wedding can be fun – they could make a joint speech, which would certainly be different!

Is it bad luck for the bride and groom to see each other on the morning of the wedding?

Tradition says yes, but practicalities may dictate otherwise. If the bride is getting ready at her parents' home and the groom at a local hotel or friend's house, this is an easy tradition to follow. But if the couple live together, are getting married abroad or are far away from home, it may be necessary for them to see each other on the morning of the wedding. If one or both of you is excessively nervous, and the only way to calm those nerves is to see and reassure the other, then that is what you must do. Go with your gut feeling on this one.

Can my mum or brother give me away instead of my dad?

According to Jewish tradition, both parents of the bride escort her up the aisle. And as weddings in general are becoming less bound by tradition, it's not always fathers who escort brides to their grooms for the ceremony.

You do not need to be given away, but you can be given away by anyone you wish; it doesn't even need to be a relative. It's a special honour and a wonderful role for someone close to you. If your father is deceased, you may want to make reference to this in the order of service or speeches afterwards, perhaps saying something like:

Thank you so much to my lovely mum for helping me through this day when we are all wishing dad could be here with us, and for taking me to the altar today and reminding me that he is with us in spirit.

Or, more formally, the order of service could say:

The bride will be given away by her brother, Mr John Brown, in memory of their late father, Mr John Brown, Snr.

I've heard of a custom called a 'unity candle'. What is this exactly?

Unity customs are very popular in the US and take many forms, but the most widely used is the candle version. The idea is that the bride and groom celebrate their becoming one while still retaining their separate identities. Generally, the mothers of the bride and groom will each hold a candle and light a candle held by their son/daughter. The bride and groom will then light a fifth, centrally located candle with the flames of both their candles. Sometimes the entire congregation will then light a candle each from the new flame. There are many different variations of this tradition, though; others include mingling two different colours of sand (actually an Apache tradition) and the bride and groom drinking wine poured from a cup from each family. You could even create your own unity custom!

Must we give favours? What do they symbolize?

At most Italian wedding receptions, you will find 'favours' of five sugared almonds, which are wrapped in netting and tied with ribbon, on the table at each guest's place setting. They symbolize the sweet (sugar) and bitter (almond) sides of life, and the five almonds represent health, wealth, fertility, happiness and a long life. In America, favours are an important feature of the reception, and very often small silver photo frames are given to guests as mementoes of the wedding.

Favours can be as unusual or as personal as you like, but obviously the more lavish they become, the more they will add to the cost of your big day. Typical favourites include tiny gift boxes of chocolate coins or jelly beans; crackers; and scented candles.

For more ideas or to buy favours, go to:
www.confetti.co.uk/confettiquette/p97

We'd like our guests to take part in the speeches. Should we set up an open mike at our reception?

This is up to you – but can quite often be a recipe for disaster, unless your guests are exceptionally talented and witty extempore speakers or amateur stand-up comedians. You also have to be confident that they can be counted on not to get too drunk!

The speech part of any wedding has become notorious for offering opportunities for guests to become bored, or worse, horribly embarrassed, and so usually the more controlled this part of the reception, the better.

The only person who can really make an unplanned speech is the bride. Many brides decide to follow tradition and therefore not make a speech, but are then called to their feet by their guests. But if your public wants you to speak so much, who could ever refuse?

? **Is it still traditional to decorate the bride and groom's suite? What can I do to avoid apple pie beds (or worse) on our big night?**

Talk to the chief mischief suspects beforehand. Make it clear that you think decorating the bridal suite can be fun but that they need to remember a few important things first. Above all, they should make sure that whatever they plan to do they get permission for it from the hotel – you don't want to end up with a big cleaning bill! Point out that you will have had a very tiring and emotional day and will probably just want to collapse into bed. You might want to drop hints about pleasant surprises they could give instead, such as scattering rose petals on the sheets, filling the room with 'Just Married' balloons, and wrapping the bed as a gift with a bottle of bubbly and two glasses in it.

Who should we buy gifts for?

You should thank everyone who has contributed to the wedding or supported you in some way. Giving gifts to the wedding party is traditional, and often takes place during the groom's speech. Gifts are given to the mothers, the best man (and sometimes the ushers) and the bridesmaids. The best man thanks the couple on behalf of everyone for the gifts. The couple may also exchange gifts the day before the wedding or during the reception.

For gifts for the wedding party, go to:
www.confetti.co.uk/confettiquette/p100

?

The church in which we're getting married won't allow confetti to be thrown, and I don't really want to be showered in paper tissue horseshoes anyway! Can you suggest any stylish alternatives?

First find out on what basis your church bans confetti. Often, its only paper confetti (and rice) that are not allowed, usually on the basis that if it rains it can make a nasty papier mâché mess outside the church! Real (or silk) flower petals are a fantastic option here – try pink, blue and white freeze-dried delphiniums for a spring wedding, deep red and orange dried petals for an autumn celebration, and silk or hand-dried rose petals all year round.

However, not all paper confetti are stuck in the seventies! There are a number of beautiful colours to match any theme out there, why not have a look on confetti.co.uk for some ideas. And if you don't want it thrown over you at the reception (it can be thrown any time, not just as you emerge from signing the register) why not slip a few pieces into your invitations?

The third main kind of confetti is metallic confetti, in a variety of stars, bells, hearts, and other shapes. This is also wonderful for including in invitations, but due to its rather sharp nature, not suggested for throwing. It does, however, look stunning sprinkled over tables, plates and the dance floor – wherever you want some glitter and shine!

Family matters

We love them, we hate them, we can't live with them, we can't live without them – families! It's a well-known fact that weddings and families don't always make the best combination. You're marrying him, not his sister, so does she have to be your bridesmaid? Are there children who need to be included in the wedding? Just because your parents are paying for the reception, does that mean they can invite who they like? What happens when your divorced parents don't speak to each other and yet are going to have to spend the day together and keep the peace? Don't worry, we're here to offer loads of advice and ideas on how to keep them all under control on your special day. A word to the wise – as with all stages of planning your wedding, don't try to go it alone. Enlist help and support from close friends and siblings. Just remember to keep talking – communication is key!

My parents are divorced but jointly hosting the wedding. My dad has remarried and would like my stepmother on the top table. My mum is very unsure about this and would rather my father's new wife wasn't anywhere near her. How should I manage the situation?

A wedding is the time for everyone to put their differences aside. It must be remembered that this is a time for celebrating the love of two people and not a battleground for others to stampede across! It's sad for the bride or groom to be in a mediatory role at such a special time, and yet it's more important than anything for them to have all their loved ones present and for there to be no tension.

Maybe you could tell your mother that it's important to you that you don't upset your father's wife and that having her on the top table is crucial. The top table is for the wedding party only, and includes the bride's and the groom's parents, the best man, the chief bridesmaid and, of course, the bridal couple. An extra lady at the table might look odd, but one way round this is to invite another person to balance the table out, for example, a brother. Having a round table can also ease any tensions about who sits where. Another idea is for each member of the bridal party (or each couple) to host a table at the reception, and to do away entirely with the top table tradition. This is the best and most sure-fire way to avoid problems on the day.

Must I let my ex-husband know that I've decided to remarry?

If you are still in touch in any way, and can bear to, you should write to him about your plans. If you have children, then you must make sure he knows before they tell him. And there can't be anything much worse than finding out at the launderette that the person you were married to for several years is now tying the knot again! Whatever the disputes you may still have, it's pretty wounding to find out indirectly that someone you promised to love forever and a day (irrespective of what has happened since) is now promising to do the same to someone else!

Am I obliged to ask my fiancé's sister to be a bridesmaid?

Although traditionally all the couple's unmarried sisters were the bridal attendants, the composition of the bridesmaids is much more varied nowadays! Before you ask anyone to be your bridesmaid, there are a few things to consider. Would they enjoy it, and do they have enough time to go to dress fittings, rehearsals, etc? Will they be able to fulfil the role of supporting you? If you want to include a female friend or relative in a role other than that of bridesmaid, here are a few suggestions:

- How about a female usher? She could then walk down the aisle in front of you with a male usher.
- What about a reading in church? This could be either from the Bible or a special poem. See the Confetti.co.uk book *Wedding Readings* for inspiration. Or perhaps she has a special talent for music or singing?
- What about a role at the reception? She could make a welcome toast or act as a mistress of ceremonies.

**My fiancé has children from his first marriage.
How do we include them in the day?**

Obviously this will depend on the age of the children, your
fiancé's and the children's relationship with their mother, and
his relationship with them. Very small children can be
delightful flower girls and page boys, and you can invite older
children to be bridesmaids or ushers, or give a reading
during the ceremony. Only you know whether they are likely
to accept or not, but it is always nice to be asked, and even
if they don't appreciate it now, they will when they are older!
The groom should make reference to his children in his
speech and thank them for their support and love, and
mention how he is looking forward to a life together with
you that includes them. If you are making a speech, then you
should include them when talking about your groom. Even
adult children will appreciate this.

I come from a huge family but my fiancé has only a few relatives. How do we solve the problem of having 100 guests on the bride's side of the church and only 30 on the groom's? I think my future mother-in-law would like to make up numbers on her side by inviting lots of family friends, but we really can't afford to.

Just because they are your family members it doesn't mean they have to sit on your side of the church. Some could sit on your partner's side. I'm sure you'll also be inviting lots of friends. Could they sit on his side?

?

We are getting married abroad. Would family and friends expect an invitation to join us for the ceremony? We know of four friends that have said they will come to the wedding and, to be honest, this is probably the right number of people. As we will be holding a reception later back at home, would it be rude not to invite family and friends abroad?

The best thing that you and your partner can do at this early stage is to decide whom you want to share this special day with you. Once you have decided, then talk to those people and express your wishes. It's a nice idea to make up an information pack that will include everything they need to know about joining you, such as: approximate price of hotels and flights, schedule of the day, examples of traditional local dishes, dress code for the day, currency, and so on.

As for the people you've decided to invite only to the reception back at home, you could send out their invites a little earlier than usual to let them know that they've not been forgotten! For example:

Jane & John are tying the knot in…. Upon their return they request the honour of your presence to help them celebrate their wedding and commitment to each other on (day, month, year) at (time, location).

What is traditional etiquette regarding who should wear buttonholes and corsages, and on which side to wear them?

The wedding party – the groom, best man, ushers, bride's and groom's parents – should wear them. This rule can sometimes be extended to include the couple's family members, but the decision is up to you. Traditionally, the men wear the buttonhole on the left and the ladies wear the corsage on the left. However, an increasing number of ladies now wear their corsage on the side they think best complements their outfit.

Who travels in which wedding car?

The bride will normally travel in one car with her father
(or whoever is giving her away). All the bridesmaids and the
mother of the bride will travel in another car (or two if they
won't all fit in one). They leave for the ceremony before the
bride and her father. The groom will usually travel to church
with the best man. This can be in either a hire car or in one
of their own. The ushers usually meet the groom and best
man at the church, as they have to make sure they are the
first people there. The parents of the bride should remember
to make arrangements for getting home from the reception
in the evening, if need be!

How do I include my father and my stepfather on my wedding day?

If you have been brought up with two fathers in your life, it's both a challenge and a joy to create a day where you can include both of them.

For many brides with two dads, the issue of 'being given away' is perhaps the thorniest one of all. Here, it's especially crucial to be true to yourself. If your stepfather brought you up, then you may want him to give you away – or if they both agree, then why not both your father and your stepfather? There's nothing to stop you. Alternatively, you could choose your mother!

How to word your invitation is another issue. One way round it is to put both families on the invitation. The wording then might be:

Mr (bride's father) *and his family and*
Mrs (bride's mother) *and her family would like to invite*
you to their daughter's wedding.

It may look a bit of a mouthful, but it means that everyone gets to be included.

At the reception, if you're having a meal with a top table, then both father and stepfather should have a seat. Don't sit them next to each other unless you're sure their relationship is good enough to take it.

If a traditional top table looks unlikely to work, then you could opt for small tables – perhaps with no seating plan or planned seating only for older guests. You will then be able to circulate and talk freely to everyone, without anyone feeling offended that they haven't been given their rightful place in the pecking order.

Although it's traditional for the bride's father to pay for the wedding, where there is a father and stepfather it may be that both will agree to contribute. It might be a good idea to list what is needed and then agree between you all who will pay and be responsible for what.

Money troubles

The church, the dress, the cars, the photographer, the reception, the food – all too quickly the costs start to add up. You want the wedding of your dreams, but you really don't want to spend the rest of your life paying for it! With a little organization and forethought you'll find you can have the wedding that you want at the budget you can afford.

Is it your responsibility to pay for everything? What can you do if unfortunate circumstances force you to cancel or postpone? Don't worry, there are ways of keeping it all under control, and you can sleep soundly at night. After all, it's not how much you spend, it's the commitment that you're making to each other that counts.

Who pays for the wedding?

In the past, according to tradition, the groom's parents had minimum financial involvement in the wedding. This is changing fast as more and more is spent on lavish celebrations. The bride's parents traditionally shoulder most of the expenses, including the stationery, the bride's dress (including her going-away outfit) and those of her attendants, transport for the bride's family and bridesmaids, all flowers (except the bridal bouquet), music during the ceremony, photography and the reception. In some cases they also cover the cost of the hen night.

The groom's major expenses will probably be the bride's wedding and engagement rings and the honeymoon. He is also expected to pay for his stag party, the buttonholes, the bride's wedding bouquet, church/civil ceremony fees, the rental of clothes for himself, the best man and ushers, transport for himself and the best man, and gifts for the bride, best man and attendants. The bride usually gets off lightly! She buys the groom's wedding ring, and that's it!

Having said all that, it's very unusual for these traditions to be strictly adhered to. Many couples pay for their weddings without the help of their families. This leaves you free to plan a wedding fully centred on your own wishes. You may find that parents would like to contribute anyway – perhaps paying for the cake or the dress – but to solve arguments, it's best to accept such offers with the proviso that you and your partners have final say on the sort of cake or dress, etc.

For more advice, register for a confetti.co.uk budget planner, which includes a guide to the average cost of each wedding item, at: www.confetti.co.uk/confettiquette/p117

?

Who pays for the bridesmaids' dresses and the page boys' outfits?

Traditionally, this one falls to the poor old father of the bride again, which really means whoever is hosting or paying for the bulk of the wedding. However, adult bridesmaids often offer to pay for their own outfits. When it comes to children you can either offer to buy their outfits yourself or ask the children's parents to pay. This cost is something to bear in mind when asking your friends if their children can be your attendants. It's unusual for children to wear their outfits again as they usually grow out of them almost immediately. For this reason, whoever is paying, it's best not to purchase an outfit too far in advance in case of a sudden growth spurt.

Who pays for the confetti?

Traditionally, guests would bring confetti to the church and to the reception to throw over the newlyweds, but these days the bride may want a specific type of confetti, for example, rose petals, featured in the photographs. The norm these days is for the bride to arrange for the confetti of her choice to be distributed by ushers and bridesmaids to guests immediately after the ceremony. Some churches/register offices do not allow paper confetti, so make sure you check what their policy is and warn your guests.

We've got a great choice of confetti on our gift channel: www.confetti.co.uk/confettiquette/p119

Who should pay for the hen and stag nights?

Each person on a hen or stag night normally covers their own costs, as well as contributing towards the cost of the hen or stag. This is why it is very important to agree beforehand on what kind of hen or stag night everyone can afford to take part in.

Should we arrange accommodation for our guests and also pay for it?

There is no tradition that says you must pay for anyone's accommodation, although if you can fit it into your budget, your guests will be delighted! Arranging the accommodation for out-of-town guests is a particularly nice gesture, and it needn't take up all your time. Sending a 'wedding pack' to your guests well in advance is one way of doing this (see page 86). In it you could include details of accommodation in the area – everything from a five-star hotel to the local B&B (if the B&B has a small number of rooms, include a few others). This will give your guests a good price scale to choose from. If you have a preferred hotel – perhaps your reception venue – see if you can make a block reservation. As long as you ensure your guests confirm in plenty of time, most hotels are happy to do this.

You might like to arrange transport for out-of-town guests from the airport/station to their hotel/B&B, and then to the church. Your local coach company might be able to give you a good deal.

? **We already live together and seem to have most of the household goods we need. But there are some rather expensive items that we would like. How can we ask people to club together?**

Most couples live together before they get married and so have already acquired the household items that would usually feature on a gift list. You can ask your guests to contribute towards one larger gift.

One way of doing this is to set up your own personal web pages. First, work out the cost of the item, open up a new bank account just for that gift and ask people who wish to contribute to pay some money directly into the bank account. You can put the account details on your gift list, which is accessible only to people who have been given the guest password. People who do contribute can leave you a message in your guest book.

For details of how to set up your own personal web page, go to: www.confetti.co.uk/confettiquette/p122

My parents have their own ideas for the guest list. Since they're paying for the celebrations, how much say do we have?

One of the first jobs when organizing a wedding is to decide on the guest list, and this is usually where the wedding party comes to blows. While invitations are traditionally sent out by the bride's parents, the bride and groom should have the chance to invite a similar number of guests. One way to do it is to split the list into thirds – one third for her family, one third for his and one third for the couple's friends.

Start by asking everyone involved to make a rough list of the people they would like to invite, then start pruning! Ultimately, whoever is paying for the wedding has the final say on numbers but, for the sake of good relations, everyone should be happy with the final guest list.

You should add the names of the minister and his or her partner to your list as a matter of courtesy, and when it comes to working out numbers, make sure you include all members of the wedding party – people sometimes forget to add themselves!

I've heard that in some cultures it is customary for the guests to pin money to the bride's dress. Is it OK for me to ask our guests to do this instead of them giving us gifts?

Asking for money is a tricky issue, although it is becoming more acceptable. People are often very happy to give gift certificates and don't see it as asking for money at all. If you have relatives from a culture that includes the dress-pinning tradition as part of the ceremony (such as Greek, Japanese or Polish), then your guests may expect to take part in such a ritual. If you are going to adopt a tradition from another culture to which you have no obvious ties, avoid taking your guests by surprise and let them know your plans. Also, if you are going to ask for money in any shape or form, it's best to give your guests some warning so they can make a decision about how much they would like to give you. The tradition you mention would probably be more acceptable in the setting of a Greek-, Japanese- or Polish-style wedding than in a very English one!

Is there an insurance policy we can take out just in case the wedding has to be cancelled?

Insurance will cover a cancellation or postponement, as long as it's not because one of you has decided you don't want to go through with the wedding! In the case of illness, for example, insurance means the wedding day can be changed without the burden of extra expense. An uninsured cancelled wedding can cost thousands of pounds, and organizing another day will cost even more money.

For more advice on managing the finances of your wedding, take a look at our finance and legal section:
www.confetti.co.uk/confettiquette/p125

Launched in February 1999, confetti.co.uk is the UK's leading wedding website, helping over 100,000 brides, grooms and guests every month.

Free and easy to use, confetti.co.uk is packed full of ideas and advice to help organize every stage of your wedding. At confetti.co.uk, you can choose from hundreds of beautiful wedding dresses; investigate our list of more than 3,000 wedding and reception venues; plan your wedding; chat to other brides about their experiences; and ask for advice from Aunt Betti, our agony aunt. If your guests are online too, we will even help you set up a wedding website to share details and photos with your family and friends.

Confetti.co.uk also runs the UK's fastest growing wedding list service, offering unbeatable choice and convenience. To select your gifts you can either go online or order a copy of the confetti.co.uk gift book. Your guests can then order their gifts by phone from one of our wedding consultants or 24 hours a day on the internet.

If you want your reception to go with a bang, the wedding and party shop at confetti.co.uk stocks everything you need from streamers to candles and even disposable cameras. It's ideal for all your special occasions, not only weddings!

To find out more or to order your confetti.co.uk gift book or party brochure, visit www.confetti.co.uk, call 0870 840 6060, or e-mail us at info@confetti.co.uk